YOU BETTER GO SEE GERI

You Better Go See Geri

An Odawa Elder's Life of
Recovery and Resilience

FRANCES "GERI" ROOSSIEN AND
ANDREA RILEY MUKAVETZ

Oregon State University Press   Corvallis

Cataloging-in-Publication data is available from the Library of Congress.

∞ This paper meets the requirements of ANSI/NISO Z39.48-1992 (Permanence of Paper).

Drawings by Lawrence Chavez IV

ISBN 978-0-87071-160-2 (paperback)
ISBN 978-0-87071-162-6 (ebook)

First published in 2021 by Oregon State University Press
Printed in the United States of America

 Oregon State University
OSU Press

Oregon State University Press
121 The Valley Library
Corvallis OR 97331-4501
541-737-3166 • fax 541-737-3170
www.osupress.oregonstate.edu

For the generation who made tough decisions to ensure our survival
For the generation who returned to what was lost
For the current generation of Indigenous youth
For our grandchildren and the next seven generations

Contents

Acknowledgments

How does one recognize the multiple communities and generations of people that supported the creation and completion of a long-term project? This book ends a ten-year project but not the relationships that allowed it to come about.

I begin by honoring and recognizing the shared ancestors and relations of Geri and me: the People of the Three Fires and our ancestral territories, Little Traverse Bay Band of Odawa Indians and Deshkaan Ziibing Anishinaabeg (Chippewa of Thames First Nation). These nations and our land bases guided us throughout the project.

Chi Miigwetch to

Geri for trusting me with her stories and every single teaching she offered.

Susan Applegate Krouse for immediately bringing me into her circle.

Malea Powell who served as first my mentor, then my teacher, and now my relative. She helped me through my grief and reminded me that this story needed to be told.

the Cottrell family, who allowed me into their house and treated me like a relative.

Geri's daughter, Jannus, who provided photos of Geri and the family.

Geri's clients, friends, and family, and her community, who have waited for the release of this book.

Chi Miigwetch to

my husband, Michael and our children Layla and Miranda; their understanding while I sacrificed our time to work on this project provided me with reassurance and love; our own journeys into adulthood and parenthood are another layer to this story.

Pamela and Michael, for their care, love, and respect.

Chi Miigwetch to my relations

including Mariano Ávila, Lin Bardwell, Marilee Brooks-Gillies, Kevin Carmody, Christina Cedillo, Matt Cox, Angélica De Jesús, Ashley Glassburn, Jennifer Fisch-Ferguson, Becky Gaan, Samantha Gaan, Heather Howard, Jo Hsu, Nicole Jackson, Cáel Keegan, Rebecca Kinney, Kimberli Lee, Daisy Levy, Braxtyn Lipponen, Santos Ramos, Trixie Smith, Natasha Stewart, Travis Webster, Sheri Wells-Jensen, and Marla Wick.

to the American Indian Caucus of *NCTE/CCCC* for serving as aunties and unties, friends, mentors, and guides on how to do the work that matters most.

Chi Miigwetch to

my colleagues in the IRIS Department for their continuous encouragement to blend boundaries, break rules, and do the work that I love in my language and on my terms.

to the academic institutions that have financially supported this project including Grand Valley State University, Michigan State University, and Bowling Green State University.

Chi Miigwetch to

Lisa King for her encouragement and investment in this project.

Kim Hogeland who sought me out, supported me, and saw this book as significant and publishable; to the entire Oregon State University Press team for their helpful feedback and careful attention.

Lastly, thank you and miigwetch to my parents, Patrick and Muntaha—the first people who taught me resilience, healing, and long-lasting relationships. For the last six years they have shown up at my house to make sure it was clean, we were fed, and the babies were cared for. Everything good from me has come from their hard work, love, and investment in the belief the next generation will have it better.

Introduction

Meeting Us at the Kitchen Table

I met Frances "Geri" Roossien when I was a graduate student at Michigan State University. Geri lived with her daughter, son-in-law, and three grandchildren in a two-story house on a cul de sac in East Lansing, Michigan. For four years, I drove down the road to visit with Geri and, sitting at her kitchen table, listened to her tell the stories of her lived experiences. I was invited into her home because she wanted someone to help her turn her stories into a book. As I was taught, when an elder makes a request like this, you say "absolutely."

This book is about relationships: the kind of relationships one has with family, with community, across generations, with trauma and recovery, with ancestral land, with writing and research, and so on. As Shawn Wilson reflects, "[r]elationships do not merely shape reality, they are reality" (Wilson 2008). Since relationships are so central to Indigenous worldviews, research paradigms, and how Geri and I understand the world, I am going to begin by offering background and context to these relationships that serve as the history, theory, and methods of the project.

I met Geri through our mutual friend and my mentor, Dr. Susan Applegate Krouse (*Ziigwam Nibi Kwe*). For twelve years, Susan was an integral part of the East Lansing/Michigan State University communities. Susan and Geri knew each other for years—serving as board members for Nokomis, the local urban native center. Geri once told me that she respected and loved Susan because she always stood for what's right, loved fiercely, and approached the world with a gentleness and thoughtful intentionality. Their relationship, serving the American Indian community of Lansing, is the foundation of this project. I came to know Susan because I read her research and wanted to study with her. In my first semester as a doctoral student, I enrolled in her seminar, "American Indian Women." Susan wanted to mentor me. She served as my doctoral adviser and invited me to work on this project with her. For a year, Susan and I met with Geri to listen to her stories. In the beginning, we recorded our sessions on Susan's old tape recorder. I still chuckle at her old-school, tested technologies. As I listened and relistened to these recordings, I noticed we always had a lot of fun together. It felt good to share space with Susan and Geri. In the tradition of urban American Indian women leadership practices, Susan, Geri, and I held multiple roles. We were researchers and writers. We were students and teachers. Geri was our grandmother and elder. Susan was the auntie and I was the youngster, who listened, observed, and learned in the tradition that young people do from older generations.

By the end of the year, Susan was diagnosed with stage four pancreatic cancer. She walked on July 12, 2010. I still meet community members who knew Susan, whether it was through providing input on the American Indian Studies program or shared activism and community programming in Lansing. Nine years later, on the anniversary of her passing, Indian Country still honors her. Even though Susan and Geri are both in the spirit world, I still think of this as a collaborative project. Every decision I make and continue to make is informed by what I know of them and their hopes for this book.

Any mistakes in the book are mine and mine alone. All successes and positive impacts are shared and reflective of the communities who raised us. It was difficult to continue this project after Susan's passing. How does one collaborate with relatives who've passed? In my writing and research, I've always been communing with ancestors who've made tough decisions to ensure I have the privilege to share my own gifts.

Susan Applegate Krouse, Geri, and Andrea standing together. We were never able to get a picture together. This is a representation of what we looked like when we first began this project.

One day, Geri called to tell me she was ready to continue working on the project. I still remember her careful tone when she asked me if I was ready. I've never been one to turn down an elder's request. Her encouragement and support as we grieved helped immensely. Geri and I completed the bulk of her story from 2009 to 2012, while I also completed my dissertation. This project gave me the theoretical and practical foundation to write my dissertation. Visiting with Geri gave me countless opportunities to critically reflect and understand how tribal nations women use the stories of their lived experiences to theorize their roles and responsibilities. After completing my dissertation, I moved two hours away and began a tenure-track job where I would commute an additional hour. Geri and I continued to stay in contact but not as often or as easily as when I just lived down the road from her. So many changes happened between 2012 and 2019. Geri watched her grandchildren grow up, travel, win awards, and attend college. I experienced motherhood twice and learned both important and difficult lessons about what it meant to be a mixed-Anishinaabekwe in academia.

In 2019, Geri walked on. During the winter, she took a fall and then fell to pneumonia twice. As her daughter, Jannus, and so many friends have said, she was ready to go. I still do not have the words to properly process the loss. Instead, I am trying to focus my energy on the promise that I made to her, which was that I would never let this project go and I would find a way for the next generation to know her stories.

Since there were three collaborators on this project, I would like to outline the purposes of this book based on our roles:

Frances "Geri" Roossien (Springtime Woman) (1932–2019) requested that Susan and I record and publish her life history. Geri is a well-known community member in Lansing, Michigan. She was a substance abuse counselor during the 80s and 90s; she worked with community members from all backgrounds, did drug abuse education and prevention in the school system, and started the first Native American Recovery Group in Lansing. Geri wanted to pass down her knowledge and experiences because she wanted her stories to serve as a resource, form of support, and affirmation that tribal nations people can overcome trauma and be proud of who they are. Her lived experiences tell us a story of surviving boarding school, moving to Lansing where she was "adopted" by a white family who kept her as a maid, becoming an alcoholic, and moving into living a sober life. She developed programming using Anishinaabeg-centered practices to heal the entire family. Geri hoped to be a model to present and future generations of tribal nations people. She wanted to tell the stories of how she survived, lived a sober life, and used her experiences to care for her community and help them survive too. In our sessions, Geri would emphasize, again and again, how important it was that more Indigenous people become substance abuse counselors and work with their communities in tribally specific ways.

As you read Geri's stories, please know that she and I had many conversations about how they should be presented. Geri had a clear framework in mind for telling the stories: beginning with her childhood and ending with her sobriety and retirement. For Geri, to end with retirement and moving into what she referred to as "Grandma care" signaled an important moment in her story for someone in recovery. She finally had the homelife she was robbed of when she spent her adolescence away from her parents and siblings. Keeping the next generations in mind and following the tenets of sobriety and recovery, Geri shared her experiences as an Odawa elder. She approached her storytelling through deep truth and critical reflection. When I came to listen to her stories, she had a clear story in mind. It was my responsibility as an oral historian and youngster to listen for the teachings and to make connections.

Susan Applegate Krouse (1955–2010) had an exceptional career as a researcher, writer, teacher, and mentor. Susan was a trained anthropologist who published on American Indian women, activism, education, and oral history. At one point, she served as the director of the American Indian Studies program at Michigan State University. Susan was so excited to work on this project with Geri and me because she felt that it was an opportunity to honor her relationships to the Lansing community and to Geri. For Susan, this book would be a continuation of her scholarship that theorizes and makes visible the leadership practices of Indigenous women in urban areas. In "What Came out of the Takeovers: Women's Activism and the Indian School of Milwaukee," Susan wrote that "(w)omen's activism, while less visible, has been crucial to sustaining Indian communities, particularly in urban areas . . . " (533).

Susan also dedicated her teaching to celebrating, learning from, and theorizing the deliberate positions and lived experiences of American Indian women. In her class, American Indian Women, Susan assigned histories like *Desert Indian Woman: Stories and Dreams* (Manuel and Neff 2001), *During My Time: Florence Edenshaw Davidson* (Blackman 1982), *Night-Flying Woman* (Broker 1983), and *Medicine Trail: The Life and Lessons of Gladys Tantaquidgeon* (Fawcett/Zobel 2000). All of these texts, whether traditional oral history projects, stories of one's ancestors, or mixed genre, highlight the experiences, leadership, and contributions of American Indian women from a relational, narrative, and tribally specific framework. I know Susan would have wanted readers to engage with Geri's lived experiences as just that: allowing Geri's stories to teach us how to listen to elder women negotiate their positions and roles and responsibilities in an urban area during a time period when it wasn't safe or easy to be an "Indian."

Aaniin, Andrea Riley Mukavetz nindishinikaaz. Deshkaan Ziibiing Anishinaabeg. Ajijaak nindoodem. Gaa-ginwaajiwanaang nidonjiba. As many Indigenous people experience, pursuing a formal and advanced education was complicated and often contradictory to how I understood the world. Even though I have always been a curious and excited learner, formal education was rarely a safe and productive space. I had not felt truly loved and accepted for who I was nor recognized for my intellectual gifts until a group of native women—Susan and Geri included—mentored me. In addition to her oral history project, Geri encouraged Susan and me to organize talking circles for more multigenerational, urban, Odawa women to talk about their roles and responsibilities. These talking circles became the content and framework for my dissertation and continued research trajectory. The grandmothers, mothers, and daughters who participated in these talking circles still have an important role in my research and my personal life.

Starting a major research project put me on a path of healing and self-realization; I needed to reconcile my formal academic training, which prioritized colonial and Western ways of knowing, with the Indigenous traditions of my community and the women I was writing about. By approaching a research project through the framework of relations and accountability, I experienced a paradigm shift that valued and prioritized Indigenous thinking and ways of knowing. Since my own family was impacted by residential schools and cultural trauma, I didn't receive consistent cultural teachings. While this is common for tribal nations people of my generation, it is still difficult to admit and interrogate. My research journey became a cultural experience as well. To write and research about Indigenous women meant that I spent more time in community, taking teachings, and feeling a sense of pride and validation that I never experienced in formal educational spaces.

Indigenous women, Geri included, gifted me with a language—a framework to understand the world and my identity as an Anishinaabekwe. I found myself carrying their stories and teachings into academic spaces like graduate seminars, comprehensive exams, and conferences. Within my own deliberate position emerged a refusal to make distinctive boundaries between academia and community—intellectual and personal. What Susan, Geri, and all the rest of my aunties and cousins taught me was to do what Native women have always done: tend to community, care for your own body, and take up space with the intent of healing, educating, and indigenizing. For Geri, the work took place in the substance abuse and urban, political sphere. For Susan and myself, it's academia. As Kim Anderson (2011) has articulated, I understand my role and responsibility reflective of my age and community standing. I'm no longer a youngster, which has been hard to admit. Now, I am an in-betweener and my role has changed. My responsibility is to be a resource, share these stories, and care for them in a way that reaches and cares for the next generation. Every day, I live my life with the purpose of being a good mother to my children and an auntie to the young people in the community, at my university, and within the discipline.

Dear reader, as you engage with Geri's lived experiences, I hope you keep in mind that for the Anishinaabeg, our stories are relationships and action-oriented. Listening is a form of participation and a prompting to tell stories in return. Since this project took place over ten years, Geri would tell and retell the same stories, including more details as she remembered them. I felt it my responsibility to add to the stories as she told them. When it came to putting the stories into narrative form, I was nervous because it felt like a moment of proving that I truly listened to Geri. From the beginning, she trusted me and my expertise and didn't want to provide much direction. Just like when any Anishinaabe get together, our process was a long one with a lot of deliberation: I would mail or drop off drafts with questions or prompts for her to read over. She would make corrections and offer clarifications by hand. We would meet at her house or talk over the phone to discuss her feedback. During these conversations, she would help me better understand her story and where it should go. This process developed over multiple conversations and different attempts of collaboration. It was never a question of whether or not I should take Geri's feedback but more of figuring out how to listen to our relationship, her expectations, and her stories to present her experiences in a way she wanted.

To tell stories in a cyclical and interconnected way reflects Anishinaabeg storytelling and epistemologies. My responsibility was to try to use our relationship to create a narrative structure where you, dear reader, could enter into relation with us. It is my hope that Geri's stories prompt readers to recall, remember, and connect with her—to enjoy visiting with an elder the way I did. Sometimes I had to rearrange paragraphs or move sections around. This occurred mainly in Part 1: Stories of Childhood, when Geri was recalling memories from when she was between four and nine years of age. I made this choice so readers could experience these stories for the first time while also sticking to Geri's request of beginning with her childhood and ending with retirement.

These are kitchen table stories. The kind told over coffee or tea and some cookies. For those unfamiliar with Anishinaabeg or Indigenous approaches to storytelling, I ask that you join us at the kitchen table and prepare to let these stories teach you something and find ways to apply what you learn to your own lived experiences. What Geri wanted was for her stories to stay with people and allow them to impact their decisions while working with the community, their families, and their health.

Listening to Your Relatives: An Indigenous Approach to Oral History

As I've said before, this project is a story about relationships. For Geri, relationships with her family and community. For me, relationships with this material and with Susan and Geri. These intertwined and multigenerational relationships inform us on our journeys and the work we do. The relationships are a part of a larger constellation of relationships where I am not at the center—where there is no center. For me, these relationships have become the methodology for being a researcher and writer—for developing an Indigenous research paradigm for oral history. I offer a series of stories as a methodology for oral history to guide the next generation of researchers and writers invested in working for, with, and alongside their communities. May these stories serve as a resource and a form of ceremony that helps us acknowledge how oral history is always a process of working with our relatives, whether it's land bases, nonhuman agents, or people from the past, present, and future.

Living in academia and identifying as a community-based researcher, I find myself in circumstances where I need to make a choice between defending the institution or caring for my community. My approach has been to be transparent and honest about the violence caused by the academic industrial complex and to admit my own complicity as someone who "conducts research." I also carry with me the tradition of American Indian intellectuals and writers who take up space and insist that our traditions are theoretical, intellectual, and worthy of use in academic spaces to make and share knowledge. In other words, I write for present and future Anishinaabek—for tribal nations people. They are always my primary audience. The wealth of research exploring the connection between resurgence, healing, survivance, and sovereignty and the development of ethically responsible and tribally focused research paradigms guide me in interrogating my role in these systems and thinking about how to imagine new options (Womack 1999; Powell 2002; Wilson 2008; Absolon 2011; Simpson 2017; Smith 1999). This project contributes to and expands these conversations by framing oral history as a relational, multigenerational, embodied, and material experience (Riley Mukavetz 2021).

It isn't a coincidence that I began this introduction with an emphasis on Geri's house or her kitchen table. For many urban tribal nations people, the house of a community elder is the site of education, safety, kinship, and healing (Lobo 2003). I am reminded of what Joy Harjo writes about kitchen tables (Harjo 1996)—they are primary sites for relationships. I grew up receiving and telling stories at the kitchen table. It's where we would meet to eat, rest, catch each other up on the day, or have a difficult discussion. At the kitchen table is where I learned important research practices such as observation, listening, and eavesdropping as the older women in the family shared secrets with each other and offered resources for support and survival. For me, the kitchen table has always been a site of teaching and knowledge creation—of communication. This oral history was created at the kitchen table, whether it was while visiting at Geri's table or working at my own table while feeding the babies, stopping to cook dinner, or spending a few moments enjoying the morning sun before heading to campus.

To understand an Indigenous and multigenerational approach to oral history, we must reflect on and theorize our traditional sites where stories are told—where they take place. We must also understand that our stories are always teachings. Since she intended this book to be for present and future generations, Geri often told the stories of her lived experiences *as* teachings. I understand the difference between a teaching and lesson similarly to how I understand Indigenous and Westernized approaches to education. Drawing on Leanne Simpson's work (2014), I see Westernized educational systems as colonial structures that are *not* based on consent, connections to the land, relationships, or roles and responsibilities. From an Anishinaabek paradigm, teaching—the nonhierarchical process of teaching and learning—is always consensual. Knowledge comes to us when we are ready. It is not something to be owned, homesteaded, or claimed (Powell 1999). For academics, this might be difficult to practice or understand, since many of us are trained to believe that success is about publishing often, finding the next and newest idea, or deconstructing the previously published.

For me, to take a teaching is a mode of inquiry that inspires continuous learning from the old to ensure the survival of our collective futures. It's about being okay with figuring out just a part of the story and carrying it on the rest of the journey. It's my responsibility to figure out what to learn from the story and not simply receiving the meaning of the story. This happened a lot when I was working with Geri. For example, there was a moment when I was on the job market and writing my dissertation at the same time. In the recordings, I tell Geri how I am trying to be patient and just see what happens. That, of course, was a lie. I would not use the word *patience* to describe myself at that point. I remember Geri taking a sip of her coffee and telling me she doesn't practice patience—instead she practices understanding. Then, she told me a story about how she learned to parent her adult daughter who was learning to parent a daughter shifting from being a child to an almost-teenager. I always understand when a teaching has been presented because I feel a noticeable shift in my body—like my shoulders softening, allowing me to breathe deeper and slower. From Geri's story, I took away that understanding allows me to be active, present, and aware of my role in the world. Geri told me that she prefers understanding over patience because patience felt too passive for her—like she couldn't control her response and had to let whatever was going to happen, happen. For someone on the academic job market, this was an important moment. Now, years later and raising two strong-willed girls, I continue to carry and learn from Geri's teaching.

The practice of carrying stories is necessary to understanding a multigenerational approach to oral history. It opens the framework of relationality to examine our connections to larger constellated networks that includes relationships with land bases and the tribal nations people of those land bases. In other words, my understanding of *this* multigenerational oral history is rooted in the territory of the Little Traverse Bay Band (LTBB): Good Hart, Harbor Springs, and Petoskey. It's rooted in the stories of American Indian intellectuals like Andrew Blackbird and the community members I've come to know and love. Even though I was born in Michigan, I grew up on the east side in an urban, working-class neighborhood. My parents rarely could afford the time or money to take us on vacation. A trip to West Michigan—to the shores of Lake Michigan—has become an experience for those who can afford the luxury vacation homes built on Odawa land. I was an adult and deep in this project when I visited Harbor Springs for the first time—using professional development money for a writing and research retreat. During this time, I made sure to visit the spaces and places that Geri recalls in her life history—and to read more stories from Odawa people of that area. Through visiting and walking the land I was able to experience the beauty as well as the devasting impacts of settler colonialism and the tourism industry. Within this methodological approach is an intention of situating Geri's lived experiences within broader understandings of Michigan Indigenous history. Her life history complicates, expands, disrupts, and confirms so much of what has been written about the Anishinaabek of Michigan.

The Role of Land-Based Relationships in Oral History

In the *History of the Ottawa and Chippewa Indians of Michigan*, Andrew Blackbird (1887) offers a Michigan Indigenous history focusing on the Little Traverse Bay Band nation. Blackbird provides the history and traditions of the Ojibwe and Odawa. Often, these beliefs are rooted in Blackbird's own experiences. What I think is significant about this text is how Blackbird makes visible a tangible shift that occurs—how the land changed—how the cultural practices changed during and after settlement. Early in the book, Blackbird remembers gathering and fishing near Sturgeon Bay. He writes:

> In my first recollection of Arbor Croche, there was such an abundance of wild strawberries, raspberries and blackberries that they fairly perfumed the air of the whole coast with fragrant scent of ripe fruit . . . and in these waters the fishes were so plentiful that as you lift up the anchor-stone of your net in the morning, your net would be so loaded with delicious whitefish. As you look towards the course of your net, you see the fins of the fishes sticking out of the water in every way. (11)

Blackbird is recalling a time and location from when he was about thirteen or fourteen years old, which would have been about 1827 or 1828. At this time, the federal government was assigning Indian agents to tribes and arranging relocation and land cessions. Later in his life, Blackbird would take an active role settling land claims—this also makes him a complicated and contentious figure in LTBB history.

I first read Andrew Blackbird's work as a graduate student in an American Indian rhetorics seminar in 2009 and continue to return to and carry Blackbird's stories. His stories help me understand the circumstances my ancestors faced during the nineteenth century

L'Arbre Croche Sign.

and help me articulate a land-based and ancestral approach to writing and research. What I realized ten years ago was that Blackbird, like Geri, wrote for present and future generations and that I was a part of that intended audience. Like Geri, Blackbird used his lived experiences to teach and prompt. It isn't a coincidence that I was introduced to Blackbird's writing at the same time that I began this oral history project and was trying to understand the role of Indigenous knowledges within my home discipline of rhetoric and writing. Knowledge comes to us when we are ready. When I hear Blackbird describe Sturgeon Bay, I feel something deep in my body to immediately visit *ininwewi-gichigami*—to experience it through Blackbird's perspective with the awareness of what tribal nations currently experience in this paracolonial world.

I believe that Blackbird wrote about his connection to Indigenous space as a way to encourage relationships with other Michigan Anishinaabeg and to prompt us to story with and alongside him. Even now, as I write and work through this passage, I feel a particular prompting from Blackbird encouraging me to visit this particular space—to stand on the beaches of Sturgeon Bay feeling my feet sink into the sand, the cool lake water splash onto my feet. I yearn to smell the sweetness of wild strawberries. Memories of fishing with my dad and uncles come flooding back. Yet, I also feel grief and anger: what it might feel like to know what the land once was and what it will never be again. These embodied reactions reflect blood memory (Million 2014) and multigenerational knowledge making. As a good relative, as an Anishinaabekwe, it is my role and responsibility to take Blackbird's and Geri's promptings seriously and experience the land through their worldviews—through my relationships with them.

In Part 1, "Stories From Childhood," Geri recalls her childhood living in Good Hart, Michigan. She refers to the same places and spaces as Blackbird: swimming in Sturgeon Bay, playing in the forest near the Tunnel of Trees, having picnics and softball games in Middle Village. I've visited and revisited all of the sites and in the process, I returned with my own experiences and additional questions to share with Geri. In one story, Geri is also speaking about Sturgeon Bay specifically from behind the St. Ignatius Church, which was originally a chapel shaped like a longhouse built around 1741—far before Andrew Blackbird's birth. When Geri recalls these stories, she emphasizes how the impact of tourism changed the lives of the Odawas. While visiting St. Ignatius, I looked at the markers, walked the path around the church, and swam in the beach. I learned that the beach is really rocky. I don't know how Geri swam in it as a little girl and neither does she. When I asked her about it, she thinks that she was so young she probably didn't care but she made sure to tell me she wouldn't have let her grandchildren do it. What I also learned was how easy it was to walk around the church to get to the beach—I was able to better understand how Geri was trying to depict these tourists, all settlers, wealthy, who didn't have the patience or care to walk around.

I would like to draw attention to the methodological importance of engaging with the land as an oral historian—to return to that landscape and try to experience the same practices of fishing or swimming or visiting to better understand the context and to form the relations that the storyteller encourages. As I write and edit, I make decisions based on my respect and connection to those shared spaces and places—I write as Anishinaabe. To do this, I need to know the land of the Anishinaabek—of my (our) ancestors. Lisa Brooks (2008), Robin Kimmerer (2013), Leanne Simpson (2014), and Louise Erdrich (2003) have also been instructive in helping me understand how to draw from one's relationship to land as a methodology for inquiry and historiography. In *The Common Pot: The Recovery of Native Space in the Northeast*, Lisa Brooks writes

> I have spent a good deal of time on the ground and on the waterways, canoeing, and in the places that I write about, usually with friends and relations, often exchanging histories of the places to which we belong. I also spend a lot of time tracking the forested marshes and uplands where I live . . . and my writing reflects this familiarity.

To be clear, what I am talking about here is not an abstraction, a theorizing about a conceptual category called "land" or "nature," but a physical, actual, material relationship to "an ecosystem present in a definable place" that has been cultivated throughout my short life, and for much longer by those relations who came before me, which for better or for worse, deeply informs this work (xxiv).

Brooks describes mapping as a tool for rememberment in a fragmented world (xxvi). To map requires us to go out and experience the land. And in doing so, it plays a role in regeneration; to create and (re)create the experiences of our relatives and ancestors and an opportunity to learn from them. Without Blackbird or Geri, the future generations of Anishinaabek might never remember the shores of Sturgeon Bay, what it feels like to swim in the cool waters of Lake Michigan, and how survival comes with so much. By returning and engaging with the land, more stories about our relationship to the land are remembered, formed, and shared. By using a land-based approach to engage with research and writing, we create knowledge that disrupts euro-centric frameworks. Indigenous approaches to knowledge-making have always been consensual, participatory, relational, and nonhierarchical. Through land-based practices, we are prompted to remember and do them again. By examining history through a multigenerational and land-based framework, Michigan Indigenous history is ancestral and embodied. We already know to listen to the land and to take this knowledge into our research; a story arises about what it looks like to survive across generations and how stories of lived experiences become maps to trace the land from the experience and perspectives of one's ancestors and relatives. I hope Indigenous folks—especially the Anishinaabek—feel a particular prompting from Geri as they read and engage with her stories. I hope that settlers reading this book gain additional understanding and awareness of the costs of tourism, public parks, and ongoing discussions of land repatriation. Maybe I'll see you at the shores of Sturgeon Bay or walking along the Tunnel of Trees in August, trying to recall what that space may have felt like before settlement.

Background on Michigan Indigenous History

Michigan Indigenous history begins with the land and the people who are ancestral to that land. The Anishinabek, who are often referred to as the People of the Three Fires, and their alliance as the Three Fires Confederacy, are composed of three Algonquin nations—the Ojibwe, Odawa, and Potawatomi. The Ojibwe, Odawa, and Potawatomi formed the Three Fires Confederacy to support and protect each other as well as offer resources. Their roles are also known as the Keeper of the Scrolls (Ojibwe), the Keepers of the Trade (Odawa), and the Keepers of the Fire (Potawatomi). The Anishinabek, with other Algonquin peoples, lived somewhere on the East Coast of Turtle Island until there was a migration prophecy. Our relatives, the Wabanaki peoples, still live along that shore. In this prophecy, they were told to follow the sacred shell and a particular waterway—which many believe to be the Saint Lawrence River—to avoid being destroyed. Some consider this destruction to be colonialism by European settlers. There were seven stopping places from the East Coast to what is now called Wisconsin, where the Algonquin people stopped or stayed. This migration occurred hundreds of years before contact with European settlers (Benton-Banai 2010).

There are twelve federally recognized tribal nations in Michigan and many more that are seeking status or who go unrecognized. Frances "Geri" Roossien is a member of the Little Traverse Bay Band (*Waganakising Odawak*). The Little Traverse Bay Band are a nation of Odawa Indians who call Harbor Springs and Petoskey their ancestral territory. In fact, their name, *Waganakising Odawak*, connects the Odawas to their home. The community members see a connection between their history and their relationship to the land. In their community history, *Our Land and Culture* (2005) the authors, all Odawa youngsters, write

> [It] is a very old Odawa language name found in old documents for the general region where a large pine tree once stood along Lake Michigan near what is now Middle Village in west central Emmet County. The tree was bent at the top and was so large that it could be seen from a great distance and was used as a landmark when traveling by water. The word Waganakising does not contain any meaning about a tree. However it may have been shortened from the Odawa phrase Waganakisi-a-mitig which means "the top of head of the tree is crooked or bent." Sometimes the French name of L'Abre Croche was used which means "Crooked Tree." The Odawa who lived between what is now Harbor Springs and Cross Village were often called the Ottawa of L'Abre Croche before about 1850. (5)

Harbor Springs is one of the most beautiful places in the world. It's also a space where the LTBB people have made great efforts to remind tourists and settlers that they are on Odawa land. If you ever get a chance to visit, you'll notice a few mile markers in both English and *Anishinaabemowin*. These markers tell the story of Odawa history before European invasion. As I visited Harbor Springs, I stopped at places like the Old Council Tree, which was a beacon for travelers to see when they arrived to *Waganakising*. Leaders and elders would meet at this tree to discuss important issues and make decisions. The tree is gone now but the sign remains to remind tourists that they are still on Indigenous land. There are also markers for Middle Village and Cross Village, which were Odawa settlements. These settlements were built as a response to assimilation and the insistence that they take on more European and American roles. Middle Village was established north of Seven Mile Point while Cross Village was built near the site of an old Catholic mission.

These settlements tell a story about Odawa history: how European invasion changed the landscape of West Michigan and the practices of the Anishinaabeg. According to past tribal chairman Frank Ettawageshik, *Waganakisi* (then L'Arbre Croche) was established as a settlement in the 1820s by the French around Holy Childhood, a Catholic mission church. The village became officially incorporated by 1881. With settlement, tourism and lumber industries became extremely present in the area and contributed to the wealth and prosperity of European settlers. Ephraim Shay, the inventor of the Shay locomotive, had a large role in both the tourism and lumber industry of Harbor Springs. In *The Indian Problem from the Indian Viewpoint* (1900), Andrew Blackbird responds to the ongoing changes of his home. As he laments, "our forests are destroyed and our game is gone" (100). As Malea Powell (2018) has argued, Andrew Blackbird wrote this book in response to the increasing presence of the lumber industry and how it began to displace Odawa people from their homes. In 1888, Ephraim Shay moved to Harbor

Area of Old Council Tree.

Springs, specifically across the street from Andrew Blackbird. By the 1900s, all of Blackbird's allotted land on the Grand Traverse Bay had been engulfed by Victorian mansions of wealthy whites who, if not permanent residents making money by harvesting the resources of the north woods, built giant vacation homes all along the shores of Little Traverse (Powell 2018). With the increase of tourists, new businesses popped up in Harbor Springs, including stores that sold "authentic" Indian goods. In his essay "My Father's Business" (1999), Frank Ettawageshik provides a history that identifies a relationship between the tourism and lumber industries and how LTBB people used their traditional knowledges to survive and market to resorters. As Ettawageshik recalls, his father owned the second Indian-owned store in Harbor Springs that sold Odawa art to tourists. Basil Petoskey, who Geri refers to as her uncle in the narrative, had the first Indian-owned store. As Ettawageshik argues,

> Art is a reflection of culture as well as one of the forms of
> interaction with other cultures. We should consider that

tourist art is a manifestation of this interaction rather than a sign of the destruction of the makers' cultures ... I would argue that both cultures have adapted to each other and that each remains equally authentic. The "tourist art" products that developed from traditional arts and became export and import items in a cross cultural exchange substantiate the continued existence of both cultures. (1999, 29)

In the nineteenth century, the United States government established and funded American Indian boarding schools. Since missionaries were somewhat unsuccessful at converting older generations of American Indians to Christianity and westernized gender roles, they began to target children. In 1882, the United States Congress passed the Indian Appropriation Act, which dedicated funding to build schools for American Indian youth. Educators believed that it was their responsibility to recognize the possible humanity in American Indians and make sure they assimilate to westernized beliefs and cultural practices. From the settlers' perspectives, these schools were considered important educational opportunities to give American Indian children education and access to Western religious and cultural beliefs that would ultimately allow them to be a part of euro-centered societies. As Richard Pratt described it, "Kill the Indian and Save the Man." From an Indigenous perspective, these boarding schools were designed to cause intergenerational trauma and implement shame of one's body, mind, and culture. Along with a Christian education, American Indian students often experienced kidnapping, physical and emotional violence, or sexual abuse. These experiences continue to impact how American Indians survive and regain autonomy from colonial effects. There were two boarding schools in Michigan: Holy Childhood Boarding School (1829) and Mount Pleasant Indian Industrial Boarding School (1891). Holy Childhood Boarding School was run by the School Sisters of Notre Dame. In 1893, Congress allowed the Bureau of Indian Affairs to withhold food supplies and rations from parents who refused to allow their children to attend boarding schools. In some cases, American Indian families hid their children so they wouldn't be taken or kidnapped by Indian agents. At one point, there were over 460 American Indian boarding schools with enrollment of more than 100,000 students (Jones, Boseworth, and Lonetree, 2011).

Scholars in American Indian studies have done extensive research regarding boarding schools, including interviewing boarding school survivors, tracing the long-term, multigenerational effects of boarding schools, and providing histories of boarding schools (Childs 2000; Lomawaima and McCarty 2006). The Holy Childhood Church and Boarding School is important to understanding Michigan Indian history and specifically the history of Little Traverse Bay Band people. As Ettawageshik observes, "In 1929, the facility was officially declared the largest Indian Mission School in the United States with 214 boarders serving first through eighth grade students" (1999, 28). The school closed in 1983. Since the demolition of Holy Childhood in 2007, survivors have shared stories of abuse, neglect, and pain while attending the school. Geri shares her own experiences and reflects on the impact of being a boarding school survivor.

In 1982, the band, initially named the Northern Michigan Ottawa Association, officially changed their name to Little Traverse Bay Band. In 1994, Little Traverse became a federally recognized tribe. Yet, federal recognition is not where this story ends. Often, discussions about the history of American Indians focus solely on the past and an interplay between American Indians and settlers. In March 2013, the Little Traverse Bay Band officially recognized same-sex marriage as a legal institution by their governing laws (Austin, April 19, 2013). This decision is significant because the tribal nation used their own sovereignty to make decisions that reflected their beliefs before colonialism while practicing contemporary Anishinaabek governance practices. As a faculty member at Grand Valley State University and connected to the urban community in Grand Rapids, it's impossible not to hear about the ongoing events dedicated to climate justice, knowledge sharing related to traditional practices like basketry or food sovereignty, and collaboration with the state of Michigan to create social studies curriculum. In other words, the Anishinaabek and the LTBB people are still here and engaging in similar practices as their ancestors.

The history I offer is partial, as context and framing to create a tribally specific narrative. While providing an Odawa perspective on recovery, survival, and sobriety, Geri creates LTBB, Anishinaabeg, and Michigan history; she employs a methodological approach to building a space for people to heal from addiction and become their whole selves. As Geri once said, "in learning to lead a sober life, I became proud of my Native American identity" (talking circles, 2009).

PART ONE

Stories of Childhood

Growing Up in Good Hart, Michigan

I was born in Good Hart, Michigan, on October 22, 1932. I was the eldest of four children. My father's last name was Gibson, but we're still not sure how he got that name. We think it happened during boarding school or when the Durant Rolls were being commissioned. We were able to trace the lineage of my mother's side from the rolls. Her family name was Kewagoshkum. When my cousin and I were looking through the rolls, we saw so many different spelling variations of our name from the 1800s up until now. We could tell it was the same family though.

While growing up, we lived on my grandmother's property. My father built a house there. We didn't live far from her and all of our neighbors were about half a mile away from us. Everyone used the same water pump except the people who had a cattle farm. We used to barter with the dairy farm that was kitty-corner from us. I remember my mother liked to can. Often, we would trade those goods for milk and eggs. In the winter, my dad made us a sled and he would put us on it. We'd slide all the way down. When we would slow down, he would push us. There wasn't a lot of space, but we would just go sailing down those hills and right down into Good Hart. Of course, there was no traffic, so we never slid into anybody, but then we would have to walk back up the hill. My dad was handy with woodworking, carving and making a lot of quill baskets. The tribe paid my father to build three buildings for the mail for Middle Village. The post offices were like one-room cabins. We used to live in a similar cabin and so did many Odawa families. When I re-

Odawa Cabin (near St. Ignatius Church in Good Hart, Michigan). This is similar to the kind of cabin Geri and her family lived in.

turned to Good Hart as an adult, only two of the cabins remained. The rest of the cabins were gone or burned down.

Most of my family lived off of Grand Traverse Bay in Good Hart. Now, this is a resort area. The tourists have moved everybody out and it's almost all mansions and summer homes. But that was our land, in the beginning, for the Odawa tribe. The tourists really took over the town. About five years ago, my cousin and I visited my brother's grave at St. Ignatius Church in Middle Village. We couldn't find his marker. All of the crosses were trampled down. I think he was buried in the part that was trampled on. The tourists would cut through the cemetery because it was a shorter path to the beach. Most of our people from the town were buried there. There is a steel fence around the church now to keep people from cutting across the cemetery to go to the beach. The tribe tried to return the plots to the original layout and appearance but had a hard time trying to figure out *who* was buried *where*. We made crepe flowers and wreaths and put them on the markers, but the names

Graveyard outside St. Ignatius Church.

are gone. Although a lot of people have been identified, there are still so many missing.

If you were to look at a map of Good Hart, it seems like it's quite a distance from Harbor Springs, but it's actually probably only ten miles. It seems like it's farther because of the long, winding roads and the heavily forested areas. On the way to Good Hart from Harbor Springs, the trees bend over each other like a tunnel. It's *really* pretty! It's now considered a tourist marker called "The Tunnel of Trees." On the drive, you can see different homes from different times in history, like Odawa cottages, farms, and summer homes. Indian Town is close by. It's about three blocks from Holy Childhood Church. A lot of Odawa families live in that area. I had two aunts who lived there. They had large families. On Sundays during baseball season, we would always get together. When I think back to my childhood, before boarding school, I can remember that we would have family gatherings, or what you would call powwows today, on the weekends. My mother used to make this fry bread in a cast-iron skillet. We liked it because you could cut it into a pie.

Tunnel of Trees.

She would just slice that up. At the time, she would use lard instead of butter. That was our butter for a long, long time. I didn't know the difference. On top of that, she would make jam to go with it. My dad would play softball or baseball with a lot of other guys from Good Hart and Harbor Springs. The kids would get a chance to run around the woods and climb trees. It seemed like we got together every Sunday during baseball season, especially when the weather was nice and they could get all the guys together. When the guys weren't playing baseball, they were traveling to find work. So, sometimes they had a team and sometimes they didn't.

All the men worked for the Civilian Conservation Corps; it was government funded. The men had to travel by hopping on a freight train to get to different locations. I remember my Uncle Basil missed getting on the freight train because it was so fast and it cut his legs off. I didn't think much of it when I was young, but later on, I thought, *Oh my gosh, what a dangerous way to get back and forth from a job*. For native people, that was the mode of transportation at the time because they couldn't afford cars. I only recently remembered this story because my cousin reminded me of it. He was gathering information about our family. He died last year. We found out that Uncle Basil was an artist. I'm pretty sure he helped my dad with his artwork as well. About ten years ago, the tribe had a showing of Odawa art at the Andrew Blackbird Museum. My uncle Mose Gibson, who was tribal chairman for a while, and his wife started that museum. We went to remember Uncle Basil and look at his work. There were collections from the different Odawa families. My daughter and I saw all these collections of pictures and letters that were spread on tables and needed to be sorted out. I know, from one of my cousins who lives in Indian Town, that the board was trying to identify people from the photographs. I looked at some, but I didn't recognize anybody. But the pictures helped me remember all of those summer gatherings and my dad woodworking. Of course, this was before my mother started drinking and my parents separated.

Holy Childhood Boarding School

I was at Holy Childhood from first through fourth grades during World War II, like 1941 to 1945. Then, I went to Marysville with my parents because my dad got a job at Dow chemical. I came back to Holy Childhood for sixth grade. I don't remember why my mom and dad sent me back, but they didn't live together after that. I first went to Holy Childhood when I was six years old. I think my mother dropped me and my younger brother Paul off. My sister Teri and brother Howard stayed with my parents. They were still too young to go to school. I don't remember if all the kids in Good Hart were sent there, but when I think about it now, it was a long way to go for school. It wasn't a typical school.

There were many sad and bad experiences while I was at boarding school. The one that sticks out the most happened around Christmas when I was seven or eight years old. I can still hear the doorbell ringing now. All of us were sleeping and it must have been about eleven o'clock at night when the doorbell rang. We could hear it from the third floor. And sure enough, one of the nuns took me downstairs and there was my dad. So my brother and I really were excited to see him because he had been traveling to find work and he came in with this big box of toys. The next day, we found out that he was taken to prison for breaking into a store. We had to give the toys back. And you know, for some reason, the nuns never said anything after that. It was kept really quiet. No one knew what happened, except that my dad visited. It was really nice of them to not broadcast it or make an issue of it . . . it was like none of it ever happened. All of these years later, it's still so clear to me: that he had *thought* to bring the gifts. He needed to bring us something because we were *there*, and then look what happened to him. He had to go to prison and that was on his record for the rest of his life. After that, I know he had a hard time getting or keeping employment. But I still think that my dad had good intentions. He must have thought that it would be exciting for us . . . but boy, oh boy! But how it ended was just so sad. That Christmas at boarding school was the only time he ever visited us. I don't think my mother ever did either. In fact, most of the children who were there never had visitors. It was like we were just dropped there and forgotten about.

At boarding school, we had no idea what we were getting into, especially my brother, Paul. He was a rascal. He was always getting into trouble. I remember they started both of us in the same grade, even though he was younger. He would do something in class or talk to somebody or drum his pencil and then the teacher would smack him across the face or take a ruler and slap his hands. I remember one time . . . I did something, I don't know what it was, and the same teacher slapped me across the face. *Oh my gosh, I can still feel the sting of it!* I mean whenever she slapped somebody, their face was red for a long time. You know, there wasn't anyone to talk to about the abuse. It was like there was a huge division between the kids and the nuns. They made us feel small and we felt so alone. There was a girls' dormitory and a boys' dormitory and then those dorms were divided for both little and big boys and little and big girls. The only thing that divided the dorms was the double doors—locked double doors.

I was in the little girls' dorm, there were four or five rows of beds and at that time, it felt like the rows were long, like ten beds per row. The nuns had their bedrooms between the big girls' dorm and the little girls' dorm. The big girls' dorm was a lot smaller, like only six to ten beds. The nuns divided us by those who had their periods and those who did not. There was no privacy, no shared closets. We had to wear dresses made out of flower sacks and we wore them for a week until they were washed. We wore everything for a week. It's probably why they gave us a spoonful of kerosene to kill off the parasites. We had the option of just swallowing it or taking it with a spoonful of sugar. It went down faster without the sugar. I imagine they used the cheap stuff too. They probably didn't care how it tasted or smelled. It had a lot of uses. The nuns would even put it in our hair to kill the lice.

At night, we could hear boys screaming their heads off. At the time, we just thought they were screaming, but when I think about it now, there was something else going on that was painful for the boys. It seems that most of the abuse took place at the boys' dorm rather than the girls'. The only instance of abuse that I can remember that happened in the little girls' dorm was this girl who was supposed to be an assistant to the nun, who had a room off to the side. We didn't think anything of it. Why would a nun need an assistant at nighttime? Who knows what happened in that one room between the little girls' and the big girls' dorm? I was so young then. I can't remember all of the events the way that some people can.

This past summer, our family went up north on vacation. On our way back, we went through Traverse City and we passed the place where my mom used to pick apples. She would bring me along and I would play in the dirt while she worked. I don't remember a lot from that time except that we lived in a little shack just big enough for a couple of children and a parent. I think this was the summer before I went to boarding school. I was so young. When I told my family about it, my grandchildren were so surprised! "You played in the dirt there?" "You lived in a shack?" At that time, my mom was trying to earn money to live on. She would get paid by the bushel and that's what she got for the day. They were paid at the end of the day. If you could imagine how much she had to pick. Oh my gosh! She picked vegetables too. I remember picking vegetables when I was at boarding school. The nuns had all the kids go outside to work the garden. The kitchen workers would can or cook the vegetables. I still remember crawling in the dirt for cucumbers or potatoes. We didn't get to eat the vegetables often. The vegetables were mainly for Sundays when our meals were a little nicer. We would get peanut butter and jelly or oatmeal along with it. Since it was WWII, food was scarce. I still remember the blackout curtains and the drills. I think about those curtains every once in a while when I hear a plane. The nuns would say, "time to turn out the lights." There was a POW camp in Mackinac—not too far from the boarding school.

Childhood Summers, Home from Boarding School

By the time I was seven or eight, all of my cousins were old enough to play together. We would spend our summers together. Sometimes, we would walk to the post office to get the mail or visit my aunt. She lived right off the water. All of those children in that small place! Of course, it was summer, so it didn't make much difference because we could sit outside on the beach or go play in the water. We would swim behind the St. Ignatius Church. Now, the beach is almost all private property. It's so rocky there. I don't know how we used to swim in that water! We would entertain ourselves by going into the water, playing by the beach, or climbing the rocks that lead up to the highway that goes up to Charlevoix. It reminds me of this place in Grand Ledge, the ledges where it's real *steep*, it was a challenge to get up there, but there are a lot of trees, so you could grab onto the tree or limbs to make it up to the top, but holy cow! Now, I would never dream of climbing that and I definitely would never let my grandchildren do that. Oh my gosh! We were unsupervised most of the time.

There was a lot of drinking going on among the adults. I remember this one sad thing that happened when we visited my aunt. When my mom and dad were drinking, all of the adults were in an uproar, especially my grandparents. My dad had started walking out into the water and he was not coming back. He was not coming back. I think one of the older uncles went after him and knocked him out and brought him back to the shore. This happened after he brought all those presents to Holy Childhood. When I went to the ceremony for Susan Applegate Krouse this past year, I was looking at a picture of a Native American woman carrying water in buckets. I said aloud, "I remember my mother doing that. I did that too." A woman behind me was surprised. She said, "Really?" They have no idea what Native Americans went through. They don't know our history. It was such a hardship for my parents. It was so dangerous to be a Native American then.

Beach behind St. Ignatius where Geri and her family would meet and swim.

My mom didn't start drinking until after Paul and I were sent to Holy Childhood. After that, the whole family changed. My dad left us—but he was always in and out of the picture because of work and things. In the summer, we went home and lived with Mother. Sometimes, we would stay with her family, the Kewagoshkum, in Petoskey. Her drinking was excessive. I grew up real fast because I had to take care of my brothers and sister: Paul, Howard, and Teri. It was no vacation for us. As a child, I didn't miss electricity! We never stayed up like people do now, watching the news at 11 p.m. I think we probably went to bed when it got dark, or at least we kids did. We weren't afraid of fires, either. They did happen, though. Both my aunt and my grandfather had houses that burned down. My grandfather's house burned down when I was around three or four. My aunt's house burned down when I was six. It happened just like in the story in *The Indians of Hungry Hollow*. The author actually talks about my grandfather's house burning down in the book. The firemen took their time getting there, and when they did, it was too late. The house had burned down. The community tried to stop it by forming a line and passing buckets of water, but it didn't work. People never considered Indians as a part of the population. I remember that when my grandparents rebuilt the house, the whole community pitched in. They used different pieces of material like tin and anything else they could get to patch it up.

My brother Paul and I had to help our mother around the house too. We had one of those yolks where we could carry two buckets. Paul, my mother, and I would go back and forth, back and forth about six blocks from our house to where we had to go down a hill; there was a pump. And then carrying those buckets of water *up that hill* and then carrying it all the way home! Oh my gosh! I don't know how many trips we made; I don't remember any discomfort in carrying that weight. It might have been that the pails were smaller than what my mother carried. They had to have been because we couldn't have managed a bucket like that.

When my mother would do the laundry, at that time, two adults and two children, we used a lot of water. She used to have the tub on the stove, and the water was boiling for the whites. This way, she didn't have to use bleach and could use the rinse water in the garden. We had different vegetables, the biggest one I remember was a big cornfield, between where we lived and my grandmother's house about fifty feet away. We used to run through the cornfield. We'd have fun in there, hiding, and when our mother would call us, we'd hide in the cornfield. We didn't think she knew where we were because the stalks felt tall. But she would say, "I know where you are!" It could have been anyplace in that cornfield. But she knew where we were. I like to imagine that the stalks wiggled because we would be giggling and trying to be quiet.

My dad and Uncle Basil would go hunting for deer, rabbit, porcupine. They hunted enough to feed our family. They didn't hunt for profit or anything like that. We used all the parts of the animal for some purpose or another. I imagine that this is how my father's crafting came in because he was able to make all of these things.

In that little place he built, he sold his and my Uncle Basil's crafts. Every time we went visiting our neighbors or family members, there was always some kind of craft going on. There was always something being made or embroidered or beaded. I imagine that it's like how some families play checkers or how the family brings out a board game. My parents would craft after supper. My father made birch bark canoes and quill boxes. He would come up with different patterns that really were clever. He would say, "I need more quills," and he would leave to find a porcupine. He would come back with quills in his hands, but he had taken care of all the other stuff outside. He had to boil the quills and sometimes, he would color them, but most of the time, it was just the plain quill. He would lay them out on a flat surface to dry out. He also carved. I know he carved these tomahawks with the big ball on the end. He would just sit there, and that's when I saw how patient he could be. Of course, the drinking kind of destroyed that. My brother and I never crafted with him—we were too young, but we helped him do different things. We just *watched* him and from that watching, we knew how to do it all. I imagine that we would have picked it up, if we weren't sent away to go to boarding school.

My mother was always *sewing*. She would make clothes for us or herself. Her stitching would last through laundry. I would watch her as she made things or took apart the material. She would make winter coats out of our old ones. She would remove the buttons and sleeves and use the same material to make a new design. She even washed and set the material. I don't know how she did that. Nowadays we use Woolite or send it to the dry cleaners, but how did she do it? She would lay the material out and use something else that we'd have as a pattern to make it bigger, and you would have a new coat, or a new blouse, or something. She was always doing that. It's amazing, just thinking about all of the little things that I remember from back then and how it could have continued if the alcohol didn't interrupt it.

When I make things for my granddaughter, they last too. The

way she jumps around! She wore a skirt today that I made for her for Valentine's Day. It has an elastic band. Everything I have made for her is by hand because I like to watch TV and work on projects at the same time. If I have an hour or a couple of hours, I either crochet or mend. I can't hear the dialogue over a sewing machine. I seldom use a sewing machine anymore. I used to. A long time ago when my daughter was little, I used to make clothes for her. Of course, when she went to school, they had uniforms, so there was only one day a month they would wear their street clothes. I was always so proud of the clothes I made for her and for her dolls.

One of my last memories of my mother was from around the time I moved to Lansing. I remember my mother wanted to buy special clothes for me, my brothers, and sister. She bought us all brand-new winter coats. I just remember my sister, Teri, walking around in this little coat, just prancing around. She was so excited. It was like the last memory I had of my sister and brother as children until we were all sent away to live with different families. I felt a huge loss because I was the one who took care of them, and of course, I was the only *one* taking care of them and that's why they were given to family members before they got into foster care or whatever they called it back then.

My sister and brother were sent to live with a family in Pellston, Michigan. They lived with them until they were teenagers. I didn't know them very well. I got to visit them one time. I always loved how the whole family was together. I don't remember much except that one of the elders was like a grandma to me. My sister learned so many stories from this family. She would tell me all kinds of spooky stories about Indians and about bear walks. She scared the daylights out of me. I thought, *Well I live here, so they're not gonna come around here.* I didn't see my sister again until she was a teenager. I would have been in my twenties. She looked for me until she found me working in Holland, Michigan. She came there looking for me. Right away, it was like no time lapsed, like we were always together. Later on, we didn't have much contact because she lived in Indiana.

I got to visit them one time. I took the train by myself from Petoskey and came to Lansing. It was a long way. By that time, my brother Paul had run away so many times from Holy Childhood that my mother kept him at home. I can't imagine what happened to him there at Holy Childhood to cause him to run away so many times. He never said anything. As an adult, he died from liver damage. He was an alcoholic too. I think that whatever happened at Holy Childhood affected him. It's so sad that he died and suffered from alcoholism. I am very, very grateful every day that I recovered from alcoholism because I went down the same path. I saw everybody drinking and for a long time, I swore that I would never, *never* drink because I saw my mother doing it. But I did anyway.

Returning to Harbor Springs

The first time I went back to Harbor Springs was when I was an adult. I went with my daughter a few years ago because the Little Traverse Bay Band held a closing ceremony for Holy Childhood Boarding School. They were going to tear the building down. We just walked right in. It was so *sad*. It was spooky, because we were going through all of those different rooms. People in the tour were telling stories as we walked through the tour. We were all remembering what we went through. It was a good thing to have the school torn down. It was, I don't know, evil. It felt awful to be there and feel the presence of all of those children who went through horrible things, who were tortured. But I, myself, didn't go through any of that. I don't know why. I don't know how I escaped that. I used to pray a lot—well, I still do—but I like to think maybe that was a big part of it. At school, I would be in bed saying the rosary until I fell asleep. It kept me distracted from what was happening in the boys' dorm. We were separated by these double doors. And, it wasn't like it was every night, but something was always going on over there. The walls were shaking, like they were being kicked. I don't know if

Portrait of Geri.

the kids were doing that or being thrown against the walls or what. But there was so much hollering. I would just mumble the rosary to myself until I fell asleep. And who knows what happened after I fell asleep. But when I went to the ceremony, I met up with a woman who attended the school at the same time as me. We are the same age. She told me about this one, big closest and it had a door with a lock on it. She said, "I remember being in there with that door locked." I didn't *know* anything about it! There were just so many secrets at that school. Who knows what happened in that room? I was so scared when I heard that story. How many other girls did that happen to? No one talked about it. The girls who were locked away just acted like it was an everyday thing. A girl got locked in the room, we would go to sleep, and no one would say anything. We never knew what happened.

The people on the tour were a little older than me. If I was in the first or second grade, they were in the fourth or fifth grade. At that time, it went up to the eighth grade. I was just so young. I didn't have the same memories. I just knew that they were disturbed by what had happened to them and they clung to themselves. Paul and I stuck together as much as possible, especially during mealtime or during class. So many kids ran away from that school and so many kids were brought back. The kids were brought to Holy Childhood for so many reasons. Some of the parents were drinking and didn't want more responsibility. That's why some of us were put there. There were kids from all over upper Michigan. Some of the kids came from families who were very Christian and strict, like my distant cousins. They were sent there for catechism training. And some kids were just taken from their families and sent to school.

We stopped in Good Hart and visited the Five Mile Creek Schoolhouse. The same schoolhouse I went to before boarding school. It was a one-room schoolhouse that taught kids of all ages, mostly Indian children. I don't remember the last time they had students in that school because it's all boarded up. Now, it's a historical site for tourists to visit. I used to think the yard was so big! But when I returned, I couldn't believe how small the yard was— the schoolhouse. The schoolhouse is probably the size of our living room and kitchen combined. While I was there, I tried to find pictures of my brother. I couldn't even recognize myself. The visit made me realize that I was so very young when I had these experiences.

PART TWO

Stories of Addiction and Recovery

Moving to Lansing

I attended Holy Childhood during most of World War II. In 1946, I moved to Lansing. I took the Greyhound bus to Lansing to meet my mother and brother Paul. At the time, my mother was working as a housekeeper. She lived with relatives. We all lived in one room—it was pretty crowded. One of the families that my mother worked for was a white, elderly couple who lived probably just less than a mile west of the house I live in now. My mother asked the lady if she would consider taking me and just keeping me for a while. So, the couple agreed and everything was fine. I mean, it wasn't anything like living with family. There was no connection or relationship. It was like, I was a servant. And so, that was pretty hard. By the time I got to high school, the couple had gotten me a caseworker through Friend of the Court. I hadn't seen my mother in a long time. I wouldn't see her until I was in my twenties. Even though the couple got money for me, they made sure to let me know that I wasn't contributing. At the time, I didn't know they even got money.

It was really hard to grow up in that house. I wasn't allowed to have any friends or do anything outside of the house. The lady who I lived with wouldn't allow me to do anything after school. For a while, I was on the basketball team and so I went to practices after school. That was really fun. I got to play basketball for a month, but I had to drop out because she had too much work for me to do. I felt so bad. The only thing I could do was meet a classmate to play tennis. We could only play for two hours, like from two to four and then I had to come home. It was the only time I was allowed to be away. I had other Saturday chores that needed to be taken care of. It was really hard to have those responsibilities. It was very different from how we raise and treat children. I think that social activities would have helped me feel good about myself. Instead, I was just reminded how alone I was. I was so angry at that woman and I felt conflicted. I had three meals a day and clean clothes. I had two skirts, three blouses, a navy blue sweater, a pair of socks, and two pairs of shoes. Some kids get much less than that. But there was just no joy there. My entire day was strictly scheduled around chores. I had breakfast at a certain time and even spent my mornings before school dusting and washing the breakfast dishes.

This lady liked to sell houses. We lived in each house, fixed it up, and sold it. I never felt like I had a home of my own and I would have to keep switching schools. We moved to downtown East Lansing on Linden Street for six months. It hardly seemed reason enough to move there! Then the couple built a house on Vermont Street by Marble School. There was only one other house on that whole block. The rest was just woods. Of course, it was farther to walk to school. The bus didn't come any farther than the main road. So, it was *rain, shine, snow*. Holy cow! All those old stories about people walking five or ten miles to school, well, this was farther!

At one point, I met this girl at school who was a bit of a troublemaker. We used to skip school a lot. One day, monsignor was coming up the back stairs of the school. We thought we were being sneaky. As we passed the monsignor, he said, "Well, have a good afternoon girls!" We really thought we were sneaky! But hanging with that girl, it was the beginning of trouble. We would go to her house because her mother worked during the day, and we'd get on the telephone and call boys. With Michigan State University being so close to home, we would get acquainted with college boys and they would come over in the afternoon. They would! We had all of these records of all the popular bands. Of course, that was the big thing then too and we would be dancing up a storm! And the neighbors would start complaining about the loud music. So that didn't last very long! Once we started cutting school, I never went back. Nobody said, "Geri, you're going down the wrong path." At that time, it didn't seem like anyone was concerned about me. I was the only dark-skinned person in the whole school and my grades were okay; some classes were good, some were bad, like math. I barely passed math. I used to hang out with girls who went to church and got all As, but I wasn't allowed to stay in touch with them. I only got to see them once and it was a big celebration for me. I just wanted to be like the other girls, act like them and be friends with them. I kept skipping until I turned eighteen years old and then, I just left school. I was told that as soon as I turned eighteen, I had to move out. I had been saving money for this for a long time but once it came, it wasn't a happy departure. I used to babysit two or three times a week, a dollar an hour until I was eighteen. I saved a lot of money up! The woman I lived with held it for me. When I asked her for my money, she said, "Do you want the money or do you want this watch?" It was a Boulevard, which was a name brand then. It had some sparklies on it too. I thought they were diamonds. I had assumed the watch was worth as much as the money or even more. I found out it wasn't anywhere worth what I saved up. I felt like I had been rooked.

I had no money and no place to stay. I was young and I trusted people. One of the priests from my school helped me find a place to live and work. He gave me a little bit of money and found me a job at a drugstore downtown. It was my first job besides babysitting. I moved into a girl's home not far from downtown Lansing. They closed the doors at 10 p.m. I didn't like being restricted that way. So I found a job at the ice cream store called Mathews and moved into a basement apartment with my friend Mary—the girl I used to skip schools with. We lived on Albert Street in downtown East Lansing right near campus. I met a lot of college kids and Mary was going to Michigan State. I started experimenting with alcohol and tobacco when Mary had parties at our apartment. It was just automatic. When I took the first few drinks, it just seemed like that was what I was going to do. I didn't stop to think: *my parents went through this and I decided I wouldn't be involved.* But after that first drink, I was just an instant alcoholic. I still think about all of this today. When I met Mary, I just wanted to rebel. That's what my alcoholism felt like. Everything that led up to my sobriety was just so much trouble.

I remember the first time I smoked a cigarette. I was by myself. My roommate smoked, but I had never dreamed of smoking. I just picked up a cigarette and I lit it, and I thought, *Well, I'll try it.* Because everyone else was smoking, and you know all around me, someone was smoking. I almost went into a convulsion and fell over backwards on the bed when I smoked that cigarette. It was just so strange to my system! After that, I started smoking little by little and it went hand in hand with my drinking. The addiction just escalated from there—drinking caused so much turmoil in my life. As my drinking escalated, I went from job to job. For the most part, I made it to work on time but most of the time, I just called in late or sick. It was just a horrible way to live and all of the people I met were just the wrong crowd. I was barely nineteen years old then.

I must have been about twenty years old when I lost my job at the ice cream store. I found a new job at a flower shop. I really loved it! I always wanted to learn how to arrange flowers. The owner took the time to show me. She had worked in the arrangement business for years. We became very good friends. Sometimes I would go to her house in Mason and have supper with her and stay the night. She must have been close to seventy years old then. She was like a mother or a grandmother to me; she was just that kind of person. I eventually moved into a small house that's still located on Grand River. It's the only house on the block that hasn't been torn down. At that time, two elderly women lived there and rented a room to me. They treated me like a special person too. They always made this delicious chicken noodle soup. They would see me coming and have a bowl for me. They made cookies too. When I'd come home, I'd find the cookies at my door. I probably worked at the flower shop for a couple of years. At one point, my uncle Mose stopped by and offered me two years of college at Michigan State University. I said, "No, I'm not interested." Can you imagine? It was just—I passed up a lot of special things in my life, not recognizing the kindness of people. I just wasn't used to it. I regretted it for a long, long time.

I decided that I wanted to leave Lansing for a while and move to Holland. I went with my friend Mary and stayed because I liked it. My sister Teri found me there. She was just a teenager and living with our mother. It was the first time I saw them since I was a little girl. We all lived together for a while. I got a job as a waitress at the Windmill Restaurant to support them. It's a famous place for the area. I really liked working there too. But, you know, the drinking affected my performance. After work, I would just go out for a drink with whoever and we would go to all the different places in town. I quit the Windmill after a year and went to work at the Greyhound station. I was a clerk there and started drinking with the bus drivers. I shouldn't have done that. I probably worked there for almost a year or two. The owners of the station were drinkers too. One time, I didn't call in to work—it was one of many times. I had been in a blackout and woke up with a stark, confused look. *What day was it? What time was it?* When I finally realized what I had done, I called them and they told me that I was fired. They said that since they were always able to get to work and function that I should too, even with the drinking. Of course, they didn't drink like I drank. When I drank it was one right after another, like drinking pop or Kool-Aid or a glass of water. It just went down fast.

Near the Greyhound station, I used to go to this dress shop. I would go in there and try on different things. Sometimes, I'd wear outfits that I got at the East Lansing Jacobson's. The owner would ask me, "Where did you get that outfit?" It was a tan skirt, with a plaid belt and a matching blouse. It was something that everyone else wore around East Lansing. At the time, Holland was still a really small farming community. He thought it was really, *really* cool. He would call me at the Greyhound station and tell me he had a rack of clothes, and to come and try some on. So, I would go in and kind of model for whoever, the designer or manufacturer. He would let me have credit and a discount, so I would walk around town looking really sharp! I would walk downtown, and it was like I was a model, everyone would stop and look! I always wonder if I missed these opportunities because of the alcoholism.

Meeting My Husband

I finally settled in Grand Haven where I lived with a Native American family. I did the housework and took care of the children. I met this family because I went to Holy Childhood with one of the oldest children. It was nice to reconnect. We didn't meet again until I was about twenty-five years old, but we struck up a friendship. She told me that her mom and dad needed help and I thought it was the perfect job because it didn't have a set schedule and I could come and go. With my drinking, it was the perfect arrangement! Oh, brother! I met my ex-husband in Grand Haven, in a bar, of course. He was also a drinker. We really had some *battles* drinking and fighting and then my daughter, I don't know how she ever survived all that! At the time, I really liked baseball and I would keep up with the games. I knew the statistics, the averages, and what games would be on and when. My ex-husband was just as interested in baseball. Whenever we were at the bar, we made bets on who would win. I won a lot! I don't remember much from this time in my life, like meeting his mother. She was born in the Netherlands—that whole area was a Dutch community and here comes a Native American into the family. For some reason, his mother seemed to accept it. I had met her way early in the relationship. He tried to sneak me into his bedroom once. His room was on the main floor and he opened up the window and was trying to pull me in. His mother was standing in the doorway and she said, "What do you think you are *doing*?" So she let me stay in his bedroom and he had to go sleep in another bedroom. She had this big house and she lived there by herself, so that's how the arrangement was that night! I will never forget it when she said, "What do you think you are *doing*?" That was the fun part and it lasted about a year.

With all the drinking, one time, he got mad at me for something and hit me and slapped me across the face. I thought, *I am* never *going to see* you *again*. At that time people didn't talk about domestic violence or anything. After he hit me, he stopped at the store and he came out with a rose. He gave it to me and apologized. I remember, I took the rose and stuffed it in my pocket. We were back together again. Probably about six months later, we got married in September, and then my daughter was born January 1964. We moved to Muskegon because he found a job working at a restaurant that served these *huge* hamburgers. They were *so* delicious. They were better than the Whopper burgers. They were so tasty. My ex-husband had just gotten out of service for the Korean War and he was living at home with his mom at Grand Rapids. He was a field cook. He told me he had to follow the troops going into battle and bullets would be flying all around. When they moved, he had to move and whatever he was cooking had to move too. I can't imagine! Holy Cow!

I started working at the Spartan Store there, it was like a Meijer only on a smaller scale and no groceries, but it had everything else: hardware, a small drugstore, boys' and girls' wear, ladies' wear. It was probably a mile or two from where he worked. I worked during the day and had started out as a cashier there. It was really challenging to be a cashier because when the lines got long, I really had to zip along. I liked to race with the other cashiers—of course they didn't know it! I did it anyway! When we went to cash out, it was always clear, maybe a penny this way or that way. But that was a lot better than some of those girls: a dollar, five dollars, ten dollars! I had to keep track of my money the old way, where you had to ring up everything, not like putting it across a grate and letting it ring up automatically. When it was slow, we would go to other departments and do inventory. I had caught on to inventory too! The manager asked me to do inventory for one section and it was all *boxes* of socks packaged up. I got through it so fast and it was accurate. He had to go double check. He said, "You did that so fast, I have to check this out." It made me feel really good about myself. He would always send me over to the girls' clothing to do inventory and I eventually became manager of that department. It came in handy because I got pregnant in April. That year I was able to set clothes aside. I loved inventory markdowns! I used to ask the manager if there was a spot to put the clothes—to hold them so I could buy them. I had all kinds of clothes set aside. The Spartan Store had just opened so everyone was new and hired together. We all got along kind of like family. They had a big baby shower for me, the *whole store* got together. That shower was *really* something; people were getting together and having fun. So, the manager asked me how long I planned on working. I said, "as long as I can, if that's okay." I worked up to two weeks before my daughter was born.

On the night my daughter was born, I went to the restaurant to wait for Bill. I was sitting there, waiting for him, and I was wiggling around in the booth. This was unusual. I didn't have any idea of what was going on because I didn't have regular visits with a doctor. There was no information on how to recognize symptoms. I just said, "I think we better go to the hospital." We were planning to go grocery shopping. He said, "Okay." So he took me to the hospital and this was probably about nine at night. The doctor examined me and said to me, "We are going to keep you." And so, they prepped me and gave me an idea of what was going to happen. The nurse kept checking on me all the time. The doctor said, "Probably another hour or so." And I thought, *Oh my gosh, that was close!* I was getting edgy and the pains were coming and Bill was holding my hand, trying to soothe me. I was laying on a gurney, going back and forth, and jumping, and the nurse said, "You are going to have to lay *quiet.*" The doctor told her, "Let her do what she needs to do." For some reason, that activity caused the birth quicker. They took me into the labor room and that was it. She was delivered not long after that. The doctor said, "That was a very smooth delivery." The labor was short—it was only from eight to eleven o'clock. She was born at 11:15 p.m. I had no idea what to do with a baby. My ex-husband had been married before and had a six-year-old son. So he had some experience. He had a lot of know-how in housekeeping and repairing cars.

One time, we stopped at his mom's house, and she had a sewing machine, a pedal-type thing. She used it as a table in the living room. But he used it! I saw him running that machine. I asked him, "What are you doing?" He said, "I am sewing up a pair of my pants." He had a little container too with a needle and thread. So, he knew how to sew on a button. I don't know how we managed to take care of the baby with all of our drinking. We'd have someone take care of the baby or we would go to his mom's house and she would watch the baby. Of course, she wouldn't do that all the time, just every two or three months. When she did watch our daughter, Bill and I would go to the bars in Grand Rapids. In one place, they said I couldn't come in because I was Native American. They refused to serve. They looked at him and said, "You could come in, but this lady with you can't. We don't serve Indians." That was the first time I was ever refused service. I had worked in a bar before as well as been in different places in Holland where there are a lot of Dutch people, and Grand Rapids has a lot of Dutch people. And my ex-husband is Dutch too. So, he got very, very upset and I just had to drive him out of there. "Don't worry about it, we'll go find another place."

Our drinking started out in a bar, but we started spending more and more time at home, drinking. The alcoholism was pretty bad and with the drinking, we would fight—sometimes arguing and sometimes, it was even worse. This one time he and I were drinking, I was disagreeing about some of the things he was saying. He tried to shove me into the bedroom and I grabbed onto the doorknob to stop him. He stepped on my leg and pushed me into the bedroom. I said, "You broke my leg!" He didn't believe me because sometimes I would joke around and pretend to be hurt or sick when I didn't want to do something. He called the ambulance right away when he realized that I was telling the truth. When he pushed me into the bedroom, a bone stuck up. He looked so scared and ran to the phone and called the ambulance. I thought, *They're gonna take me to emergency, set me up, and put a cast on and take me back home.*

They kept me for almost three weeks because they had to do surgery. There was a splintered bone. They had to put all kinds of pins in my leg and then they had to make sure I could get around on a hip cast. The nurses would take me up and down the stairs and up and down the hallways. I had to do that for two or three days and *then*, trying to go down the stairs with a cast on—I couldn't bend. But that was scary looking down those stairs. It was like, you got to do it or you don't go home, and I wanted to go home. But, during that time, Bill came to see me every day and either brought flowers or fruit. Later, I learned that this was called the gift giving or honeymoon period of the cycle of violence. At that time, the hospital didn't even ask how I fell and broke my leg. Things were very different then. I remember we were in the emergency room and he gave me his wallet because he had just gotten paid. He said, "Take this and keep it and pay for whatever you need." Of course, I didn't. I said, "We'll have to figure it out after all this is done."

When I returned home from the hospital, my mother-in-law came to visit us. She stayed probably a week to take care of me. She made sure I was able to get around. That's when she decided that we needed a house of our own because we were always renting. She said, "I will take you to look at all the houses you need to look at." There must have been about twenty houses we scheduled to look at. We'd go into each one and look around over and over. I was on crutches at this time, but I was able to move around pretty good by that time. Eventually, we found a house near Holy Cross Elementary School on the west side of Lansing. We enrolled our daughter there. At that time it was safer for kids to walk back and forth to school. And there were a lot of kids who went to Holy Cross, and that whole area was a *very, very* safe place to live. Later on, it got too scary to live around there. At the time, I stayed home while my husband worked. I would do things with our daughter's class like show them how to make doll clothes. The girls would walk over from Holy Cross to our house. All these little girls in uniforms come walking up the street! I bet the neighbors would be wondering where all these girls were going. They were in lines with Catholic school uniforms. They were so cute! Bill would set up tables in the living room, and we had a little, like a little library, and there was a table in there and you could spread out the materials.

Bill and I were together until our daughter was eight years old. The violence didn't really stop. My daughter and I had run away so many times from him—we'd gone to different places. I worked at Howard Johnson's and the manager transferred to a new Howard Johnson's in Indiana. He said that he knew of all the troubles I had, and that I could move there and work for him. This time, I was gone for nine or ten months, almost a year, and then Bill found us. I asked him, "How did you ever find us?" He would get time off work and he would go up and down the different towns and look around, and started moving inward toward Indiana. Of course, we were just over the line of Indiana, and so he talked us back into coming home. And we did. It wasn't long afterwards that the fighting started up again after a couple of months. So we left again and it was permanent. I was *not going back.* I think he knew that. He had a job offer and wanted to move to California, and I said, "No, I don't want to go." So he said "Okay, you stay here." So I had the house and he went to California and stayed there for a long time. It was a relief. My mother-in-law turned out to be very, very supportive of me. Even when I stopped drinking, I didn't call her for three months until I was sure I was staying sober. When I called her, she was so excited that she came and drove to see us that day and took my daughter and me out to dinner. She must have been in her seventies because she retired, and she drove all over and took vacations in Florida and even Texas. So we never did know where she was going to be. She used to come visit us every couple of months and see how we were doing.

My background and experience with alcoholism and domestic violence helped when I started counseling people. I knew all the referral services because I used them when I was in the 12-step program. In fact that's how I got my job—one of the members in twelve steps who worked at one of the big programs referred me. Talking about my experiences with alcoholism reminds me of one of my clients. I do consulting with Michigan Indian Employment and Training Services. Every once in a while they call me and want me to talk to somebody. It ended up being someone who used to attend one of my classes for the Native American Recovery Group when she was a little girl. Her mother attended the class and used to bring all three of her daughters. Now, they are all grown up and the middle sister was concerned that her younger sister might be an alcoholic. Her family was splitting apart. The boyfriend went to jail—just a bunch of unfortunate things. She wanted to talk to me about how to talk to her sister. The girl said that the class taught her and her sisters to notice the signs. They watched their mother struggle with alcoholism and cocaine and all decided they would never be involved with drugs or alcohol. It's like when I grew up, I witnessed drinking from my parents and grandparents, and even some of my cousins. Like the sisters, I had decided that it was one thing I would stay away from.

Seeing My Brothers Again

I wanted to make sure that I talked about my brothers. They also witnessed the alcoholism in our family. They have both passed away. Howard was the youngest boy. I didn't know him very well because he was still a baby when I was sent to boarding school. My mother gave Howard and Teri to relatives—the same ones I lived with in Grand Haven when I was in my twenties. Teri and Howard were around five and three years old. Almost ten years ago, my sister Teri contacted me. She called to tell me that Howard died in a knife fight in Chicago. I guess she found out because he didn't contact her during Christmas. They had an agreement to always reconnect around the holidays. They would send cards, meet, or even call each other. She hadn't heard from him in two or three years. She found out from one of our cousins—the one who helped me put crosses on the graves at Holy Childhood. He died recently too. But he died sober. He was such a good person. His wife was injured in a car accident and he always took care of her. I went to his naming ceremony. It was held in their backyard. It was just beautiful. I can't pronounce the name in *Anishinaabe,* but it translates to something like "when you hear the rustle of the leaves, you'll think of him." If you stood in his backyard, then you could see how it opened onto all the mansions across the lake. The area is still such a mix of small Odawa cabins and homes and then mansions. When I was at Holy Childhood, the nuns would take us on these walks past the mansions. Maybe to show what we could have. But they didn't think about how that was all of our land. Those mansions have just completely surrounded us. Teri would always call Howard "Beanie." She told me that he was really mischievous and always up to something. I met him when I was living in Holt. I was still married then. He was passing through on his way to Chicago. He stayed a couple of days and we just drank. I would usually wait to really drink until my husband came home. But Howard would just drink and drink and drink until he passed out. It wasn't a good way to remember him. I think it was the last time I saw him too.

I was much closer to my brother Paul. He was closer in age and we went to boarding school together. He was really smart. He ended up living with my mother in Muskegon because he ran away from boarding school so many times. As a teenager, he liked to work on cars. He was always tinkering around. I remember visiting them one time and asking him, "Don't you have to do some studying?" He would say, "No, I'm alright." He barely ever had to look at a book. He always got all As in school. I was always so jealous. He must have gotten into trouble of some sort because he never graduated. He stole something with a group of his friends. He ended up with a record and would come and go. At one point, he moved out west with a girlfriend. They had children together. I didn't even know who she was. Their children could be members of Little Traverse as well. I don't even know how old they would be right now, maybe around my daughter's age.

I started sobriety in 1975 and it must have been about that time when he called me from Cleveland, Ohio. He said he had been drinking with some friends and they drove him to Ohio and they dropped him off because he didn't want to go any farther. He wanted to get back to Chicago but he was having trouble with his leg. I didn't have any money to help him out. He asked for a bus pass. I made a lot of phone calls and found a traveler's association and that helped him get to Lansing. He was pretty sick by that time. I said, "If you stay with me you got to stop drinking." He registered with social services and Medicaid so he could take care of himself. He stayed with me for about six months. I asked him to go to AA once a day. And he did. He started to make friends and he moved in with one. His roommate started drinking. And so Paul did too. He started drinking and I asked him if he wanted to stay with me—to start to go back to meetings. He said "No, I'll think I'll go back to Chicago." He wanted to go and see a woman and drink with her. Women were always drawn to him.

In April, I got a phone call from a hospital in Chicago. They received a phone call about Paul. He was found on a cot surrounded by whiskey bottles. At the time, he was diabetic and had cirrhosis of the liver. He was in a coma and they needed to know if they could amputate one of his legs. I said, "Go ahead." They thought that would help, but it didn't. They called again and they wanted to do something with his heart, like cut it open or something. I said, "Go ahead." I called to find out what happened. They said that he was getting worse and if I had any way of getting there that I should come now. I didn't, then. I was living off of social services and food stamps. Later that day, he died. I thought, *Oh, if only he would have stayed and continued his sobriety instead of going to Chicago with that girl.* The AA meetings helped with this too—the grieving of my brother. So many people shared stories of losing a loved one, especially when alcohol was involved. The people in AA would come up to me after and comfort me. It was really hard, especially after he had called me for help and was sober for six months. He was so close. He was getting help. I don't think that his roommate even knew what happened to Paul.

I was really sad about Paul for a long time. He reminded me of my father. He used to work on cars too. After Paul went away to find jobs, he finally bought a car. It was an old one of course. So, he had to repair it and take care of it. My son-in-law works on cars too. With Howard's death, for some reason, it didn't even register that he was my brother. I couldn't remember him in my life. I didn't have that same connection like I did with Paul. The 12-step program really helped me understand my grief not only for their deaths but for not being close with them. I would hear people share their stories of losing a loved one to alcoholism. During the 12-step meetings, members would come up after and comfort me. I kept thinking about Paul's roommate, the guy who started drinking again. I didn't know what happened to him. I guess he just kept on drinking.

But, all of this—what happened to Howard, Paul, and my cousin—helped me stay in touch with my sister Teri. Before this, I didn't know where she lived or what her circumstances were. So we got reestablished. She came to visit me. She had been married for quite a while. She tried to find out more details about where Howard was buried but she didn't find much. You would think the hospital would have some records. But we never found him. For a while, she lived in Gary, Indiana. We went to visit her a couple of times. She has a nice house and a nice backyard. Eventually, she moved down south because that's where her husband is from. She and her husband would visit a couple of times a year to play the casinos. Usually, they'd win! One time, she even won enough money to buy a brand-new car. When I start thinking about wanting materials things, I realize that it's not the most important thing in life. Like I've said before, I thank God for every little thing even when I think negatively. Like, "Oh, this weather is awful!" I say, "Thank you God that I don't have to drive in this weather!" Living a sober life helped with this—these thoughts.

Starting the Path of Sobriety

I remember there were some neighbors probably two blocks away and they were having a gathering. I went there and started drinking and I had a blackout. I started home around seven or eight at night. It was raining; our driveway always got muddy when it rained, and I had fallen in the mud! So I was *all* covered with mud when I went into the house. I don't remember how I got into the bathtub, but I did, clothes and all! You know, there were all these little things like this that happened when I drank. But it never stopped me. When I stayed home and drank, I would get on the phone and talk, *talk, talk, talk*. Anytime of the day, anytime of the night, I would be *talking*. I used to drink beer. But when I couldn't stand the taste of it, I switched to wine. I would mix it at first with 7UP. At one point, I just drank straight wine. Since it was sweet, it was easier to drink so I ended up drinking more than when I was drinking beer. This one time, I remember sliding off a stool in the kitchen, just *sliding* off. It didn't feel like it hurt when I hit the floor and I don't know how long I was there for because my daughter was watching television. I was probably lying on the floor for about a half an hour. After that, I thought, *I have to get some help.*

By this time, my daughter was in the fifth grade. She was friends with a girl from her class. Her mother and I were close because we would get together and do school projects for our daughters' class.

I remember one time I told her, "I think I am an alcoholic. I think my drinking is becoming a problem." She knew the whole time, but she never mentioned it or brought it up. She said, "My brother goes to a 12-step program." I started to see how we were all connected, especially when I decided to ask her for help and talk about it. She called her brother and he had this lady call me who had been sober thirty years at that time. By the time that she called me, I was already drinking. She said, "Tomorrow, just remember don't take the cap off the bottle." I thought, *Is that all I have to do?* I realized much later that it was the only thing to do. Don't take the cap off the bottle.

I continued drinking that day and the next day, I thought, *Well, why not?* And I didn't drink the *whole* day. I thought, *OK, I'll try it the next day.* And the next day I didn't. In the meantime, I would call a woman from St. Lawrence Hospital to check in. She asked me to call her and let her know how I was feeling. She would ask me routine questions like "How are you doing physically?" We talked about whether I should stay at home or if I should register for an inpatient substance abuse program at St. Lawrence Hospital. She said, "Well, you went over two days without drinking." That was a good thing—even if I didn't realize it at the time! But she still advised me to come in and stay for two weeks. I thought, *Well, I can't do that. I have a daughter at home.* So, I stayed home for seven days and I didn't drink.

This lady said, "When you are ready to go to a 12-step meeting, let me know, and I can pick you up." So I called her that Monday; this was a week after I had stopped. She said, "Well, I can't do it." I thought, *Oh* no! *Here I am, ready to go, and she can't because she was speaking at another meeting across town.* She said, "But I can get you somebody else." I said, "Okay." All that day, I thought, *Do I want to meet this other lady?* I felt comfortable with the woman who I was speaking with on the phone. I kept wondering if I could follow through. I would have to wait until seven at night when she would pick me up. I thought, *Well, just one more hour, I made it this far, five minutes more, I can make it!* And sure enough, there she was! This lady had been sober two years, and she took me to my first meeting, and it was a *big* meeting. It was like three of those long cafeteria tables, and people were sitting all around that, and they were sitting around the wall. It was so crowded, and I thought, *Oh my gosh! All these people are talking.* They started going right down the line to make sure they got everybody. The lady I went with, I hid behind her because I didn't want to talk. I was there but I didn't want to talk. I just wanted to listen. So the chairperson just went on to the next person, and I thought, *Wow, that was a big relief!*

The lady I had been talking to became my sponsor. After that, she picked me up for meetings every night. I got to meet so many people with sobriety and they all had so many different experiences. It was good guidance for me to see people with many, many years of sobriety. They knew the simplicity of *just being.* At other meetings, it was very different. Some people would pound on the table. "You got to do this!" or "You got to do that!" It scared the living daylights out of me. I started to go to two meetings a day. But, when I would go home, it was this big, empty house. I could hear everything that was going on. The little cracks—things like that. You know, it was so quiet. I wasn't used to that, being by myself, *completely by myself.* I would get home from my meetings around one o'clock and was just so helpless. I had no idea how to do or be anything. To this day, my daughter swears that I used to burn everything I cooked. In those early days of recovery, I felt so lost!

I told my sponsor about how hard it was to be alone after the meetings. She suggested that I walk up to St. Lawrence Hospital because it was so close to my house and get acquainted with whoever's there. So I did that. I met all the staff and talked to some of the residents, where eventually, I started going to different groups in addition to my two meetings a day. At one point, they asked me to be their representative. I was supposed to represent the community at St. Lawrence. I would speak on their behalf. One of my responsibilities was to see if they could re-establish meetings at St.

Lawrence. So with me going there, and knowing the staff, I checked into finding out if we could have a meeting there every week. As a result, they set a time. I called my sponsor and she said, "Get as many names as you can of people in sobriety because if you need to talk to somebody, you are going to need one of those people to talk to." It's true. One day, I wanted to go to a day meeting and the person I usually rode with couldn't make it. I called ten people on that list. And none of them were going to the meeting. They had other things to do. The tenth person I had called, it was the attorney general's office, and I said, "I think I have the wrong number!" I dialed it again, and thought, "Heck, I will ask for the name of the person with this phone number." It was one of the lawyers. When I heard his voice, I recognized him. I sat beside him in the day meetings. I said, "This is Geri, I need a ride to the meeting, are you going?" And he said, "Sure, I'll pick you up." It was the right number. People in sobriety come from all walks of life. It wasn't until much later that I would realize I made my own residential treatment. I couldn't go to St. Lawrence. So, I had to figure out something else.

On Faith and Spirituality

I never realized what spirituality was until I stopped drinking and started the 12-step program. I had heard in the meeting, time and again, that I just had to keep coming back and focus on the next steps. People talked a lot about reading the "24-Hour" book, the "Big Book," and talking to sponsors. I always had a lot of questions, but I was never able to talk about them because I was too withdrawn and scared. So, I followed up on a one-to-one basis. My sponsor, my one sponsor pointed out to me that I had been sober for *so long,* for three months or four months. She said that something is working for you. You always hear in meetings how people select different things to be their higher power. I remember this one guy had selected his truck to be his higher power! Or a tree was a higher power. It

Geri and Ned Krouse.

was anything you wanted it to be. So I heard a lot about how people graduated higher powers to higher powers to higher powers until most of us believed that God was the higher power. But we never said that at meetings because different people had different beliefs and religions. So we just said "higher power." I started reading the "24-Hour" book every day and gradually got the idea that there were a lot of things changing in my life. I started to make a gratitude list like it was suggested. I became so thankful for anything that came along especially that I was doing all this sober. And a lot of great things were happening compared to what life used to be like. It was something to really look at and say, "This is really something I never would have done if I didn't find a higher power."

I had the seeds of spirituality. But I think attitude has so much to do with it, and past experiences. I had to work through it all and see the parts that spoke to me and didn't. At Holy Childhood, it was always about discipline and punishment. Somebody shaking their finger at us saying, "You do this," or *whack*—a slap across the face. Some kids got disciplined to go to bed without supper. We never got that much to eat, and to send somebody to bed without supper

. . . It was just one of the things that I don't use or need. But having a good attitude, I think, is a way to see change and move forward—to do things. I looked at a lot of the big things that were happening in my life.

Like when I was first starting out as an intake officer at Cristo Rey Community Center, I wanted to go to a Native American conference about sobriety and addiction. It was one of the first conferences to specialize in Native Americans. And this was at about a year and a half of sobriety. I began to notice that there weren't any other Native Americans who attended regularly in the meetings that I went to. I wondered if there would be anybody else at the conference. When Native Americans did come to the meetings, it was rare. It almost felt strange to see them! I remember seeing one man come every once in a while. He was staying sober. We became good friends. I still know his family—his sisters. Another man came and went. It just never worked out. It seemed like they would try a meeting but it wasn't what they wanted. I had the same feeling myself. When I went to the first meeting, I remember thinking that it was not going to work. But I kept going. I started to see what spirituality was—it was a feeling about being able to do good things and say good things. Even where there are a lot of times when you don't feel like it!

But I couldn't afford to attend the conference. I found out that someone paid my way. The person who told me said that the donor does not want to be known. It was for the hotel, registration, and my meals. I was so excited. One of the members loaned me a suitcase. Then, I realized that I didn't have any clothes. All I had was one pair of slacks, a pair of shorts, and a couple of tops. That's all I had, but I kept rotating them. I was going to meetings wearing the same thing every day. This girl, another member, she asked me if we could talk after one of the meetings. She told me that she liked what I had said at the meeting. So I sat down with her and she told me that one of her problems was that she was never able to finish a task. She said, "I have a whole trunk of clothes in my car that have been in there for over a month and I haven't taken them to Goodwill!" I said, "What size are they?" There were two big bags of clothes. There was nothing wrong with them! There were so many things, suits and sweaters. There was a lot of clothes for me and my daughter to wear. It was like I was in the right place at the right time.

I still can't believe how different life is now. There are a lot of things that I don't do according to Catholicism or how I grew up as a Catholic. I think that boarding school really impacted what I thought about in terms of spirituality for a long time. I like to use the Lord's Prayer though—maybe not the serenity prayer. I think it's important to just remember to say thank you, to say it at the end of the day. When my granddaughter was young, she said prayers for all kinds of different things like the dogs or cats of the neighborhood. It's really cute. Keep it simple, that's what they say, keep it simple. I really like listening to her pray for the trees especially.

The other day two eagles flew over my house. My youngest grandson, his spirit name is "little eagle," and he is very alert when it comes to eagles. I picked the kids up from school and we saw the eagles as I pulled into the driveway. I hardly had time to stop the car because he *jumped* out of the car. He said, "There are two eagles," and of course when I saw them, I jumped out of the car too. They kept going around and around the house and you know, I would say if they were going around the neighborhood, but *right around the house*—it was amazing. My grandson ran into the house to get a camera but they started going off to the west and he couldn't get their picture. He stayed on the porch for a while hoping they would come back, but they were gone. They just came to visit for what must have been five minutes. It was just so exciting to see because the last time I saw eagles was when I went with the elders to the National Indian Education Association Conference. On our way back, the elders looked out the window and they saw an eagle and clamored to the side of the bus and watched the eagle flying. They said that the eagles were watching over us. This acknowledgement of the eagles as guides is a part of spirituality too.

Many people have asked me how I am able to combine both Native American spirituality and the spirituality of the 12-step program. I see a lot of similarities because both are according to how I feel inside. With the steps, I've heard people ask, "How do you describe the steps according to Indian tradition?" So, the first step is something about acknowledging when life became unmanageable. I think this is the opening to spirituality—any spirituality. There's the twelfth step, being able to take the message to other people. I think that many Native Americans do this now with their beliefs and practices—with the Native community. I think that spirituality is about how you behave and how you treat other people and accept people as they are. I remember one client came in and he had been drinking. Now, the rule was if the client had consumed any alcohol, then they had to reschedule their appointment. But I saw this person anyway. Nobody else knew about it. He was a Native American and kept coming back just because I took the time to see him. If he had been turned away, he would have been a lost person. He might never have come back.

This happened to a lot of our Native clients. I like to try to bring examples from my own life into my classes, especially about relationships and understanding. One client was having difficulty with children who were misbehaving. I always like to ask clients to put themselves in the child's place or think about their unwillingness to do so. When I draw with my granddaughter, I like to point out her strengths. She's a much better drawer than me. I say, "See, you are doing a better job than Grandma." That kind of a thing. One time, my daughter—she was always so mischievous. When she drove from the University of Michigan, sometimes she would wait out in the parking lot because I would be out in five minutes or so. This one time, I was walking out to the car, and bam, I got hit in the face with this water. She was shooting at me with a water gun. So there was no way to retaliate. The next day I bought a gun that was bigger just so I could see the look on her face.

When I first stopped drinking, I would go home and I was just listless. I didn't know how to do anything—not cook or keep house. One night, I decided to sort out an upstairs closet. So I pulled everything out. I found a box that was my ex-husband's. It had all these letters that I had written him or cards that he received—just a lot of personal stuff. I found a few books. I couldn't believe it. I found a copy of the "24-Hour" book. He had tried to get sober. That day, I had prayed for the "24-Hour" book and the "Big Book." I didn't have the money for them. And in that box, there was both and a message from his sister on the covers. So I took those books and I read. It was like when my sponsor had gotten me a subscription to a book put out by the central program in New York. I would get the sofa all ready with the pillows set up and a cup of coffee and just read it all the way through. I found the books about three or four years into my sobriety. I was just talking to my daughter about this. My ex-husband died a few years ago. He had a bad heart for years.

One time, he had a heart attack on the side of the road while driving home from work in California. He stopped his car on the highway, got a pillow, and then laid down on the side of the road. A car came along and called an ambulance and got him to a hospital and he survived. That was ten or fifteen years ago. It was just gradual deterioration. So he has been hanging on for quite a while. He eventually moved to Florida. When he lived in California, he would call me when he was drunk. By that time, I was sober so I made sense and we didn't argue anymore. I didn't tell him that he was drunk or hang up on him. He would talk all night, till like one or two in the morning. I would fall asleep and be like "uhhhuuh" or "hmmhmm." I thought, *Well, he is paying the phone bill*, but those conversations led him to consider sobriety. One day he called me. He had been arrested for drunk driving and he was placed on probation. He was ordered to go to AA meetings. He called me and told me that his probation had ended and that he didn't have to go to AA meetings anymore. He said, "I don't have to stay sober but starting tomorrow, I am going to." And that was it. He stayed sober on his own without any kind of support group.

In the meetings, we cover one step per week. They advise you to have three sponsors so you could talk to them and ask questions. I didn't talk in the meetings for probably about six months. It was *scary, really* scary. If I got to a meeting and listened, that was it. It was enough for me. I would talk to people after the meetings because I could do one-on-one a lot easier instead of sitting in a large group and talking about sobriety. They would talk about so many things, like how they recognized that it was time to quit. Those types of conversations were helpful for beginners like me to express what was going on in my own life. It was their experiences that helped us.

There were so many different types of stories. Some were funny, some were scary, some were sad. It just depended. One guy would tell us stories about his days when he used to drink under a bridge. His tennis shoes would get holes in them and rusty because he would wet his pants so much. I've heard so many similar stories. When I met this guy, he was sober for at least fifteen years. These recovery stories helped me think about my own sobriety and experiences. Reading the "Big Book" and the "24-Hour" book every day helped me focus on my sobriety when I wasn't in meetings. Both books really helped me think about my own experiences. You have to focus on recovery to stay sober. When I would start to have feelings of doubt, I would call my sponsor or read the "Big Book." That's what you were supposed to do. One night after a meeting, I came home and my neighbor, who was watching my daughter for me, told me she got into a fight with another neighbor. The neighbor called her the n-word. I could have used that situation as an excuse to drink. I wanted to! I must have talked to my sponsor about half an hour to get over this. But that was why we had those phone numbers handy. I think the sponsor came over to my house too and stayed with me for over an hour, understanding I was so upset. It was just crucial to have someone with sobriety in my life. Once

I was in recovery, there were a lot of happy things that happened after that, so many happy things.

I've always had some kind of celebration on my sobriety anniversary because I think it's something to celebrate. A lot of people don't. They just consider it as another day. They take it one day at a time. When I was younger, I used to go to Big Boy and have the chocolate cake with whipped cream. Those were good memories. I'd have like six people with me. For a couple of years, I would have anniversaries at Cristo Rey and those were big, like almost sixty people. One year they had a podium set up so people could talk about their sobriety and how they knew me. My boss and his wife would come too. A lot of the people from the Native American Recovery Group would come too. It was a big gathering. People would share stories about their sobriety. Our neighbor has been sober for a long time but not as long as me.

Susan Applegate Krouse was at my last sobriety gathering. She was there with her husband. He had a show in Mt. Pleasant and she thought he wasn't going to be there with her. But then he showed up! She was so surprised. She was a lady. I have so many memories of being sober and celebrating that I cannot say what was my favorite one except that it was another year and that my family is supportive of me. I didn't start incorporating the American Indian traditions into my anniversaries until I moved into this house with my family. The backyard is so beautiful. My son-in-law made a pit and we could celebrate with a fire. We would ask people to bring a dish to pass. Oh my gosh, there was just so much food. If I had enough money, I would ask our pipe carrier to have a ceremony. Then, we would eat and mingle. The part that I liked the best was the ceremony. Our pipe carrier did a good job explaining how sobriety was connected to American Indian beliefs. I really liked these celebrations because it would be an opportunity to see people that I haven't seen for a long time.

PART THREE

Stories of Working with and for the Community

Working with Clients

While attending meetings in the 12-step program, I made so many good and lasting friendships. One of those friendships was with an ex-marine. He had fifteen years of sobriety and he worked with a really big substance-abuse organization. We had been in the same meetings for about five years at the time. He knew that I had made good progress, but I *still* did not speak in meetings. So he would take me aside to talk to me and joke with me for a few minutes before going back to work. I think he did this to try to get me to feel more comfortable. One time he told me that Cristo Rey was interviewing for a secretary for a new substance-abuse program. At the time, I was taking courses at Davenport University to be a legal secretary, so the job seemed like the right fit. My friend even wrote a reference for me. My interview was only supposed to be twenty minutes and it ended up being two hours! It just felt like we could talk forever. The coordinator, the man who interviewed me, worked for human resources for the city of Lansing. He asked all kinds of questions about my sobriety and how I was following the twelve steps and how they were working in my life, and it just went on and on. I realized later that he was asking me these questions because he thought that I could help the clients. He told me I would start off as secretary to get to know the program, and then in January, when the funding came for a Native American counseling position, I would be ready. So he hired me that *day* before I left, and he asked me if I could start tomorrow. But I already had a part-time job. I don't remember what I was doing, but I said I had to give at least two weeks notice. I was also studying at Davenport University. I felt conflicted on whether I should finish my education or take the job. I went to see my friend, the ex-marine and his wife. We were all really close. After meetings, we would go to their house for coffee. There was always a big group of us! He became like a sponsor for me, but we were more like buddies, I guess. And so I said, "I have a predicament; I've been offered a job." I described what I was doing, and told him, "I don't know if I should accept this job or stay in school." He said, "What are you going to school for?" He already knew. He's heard me talk about it. It's all connected. I was going back to school for the exact job I was offered. So I called the coordinator the next day and told him I would accept the job and could start full-time in a week. The woman I worked for encouraged me to take the job too because she knew I was a single parent and this would be a better position for me.

So I went to work at Cristo Rey, and at that time I was typing eighty words a minute, can you believe that? I can't even type ten words a minute now! But the coordinator was so fascinated with my typing skills. He would always come by and look over my shoulder. I would be like, "Wait a minute, this kinda makes me nervous." He'd say, "Okay, I won't do it!" So he'd back off, and then the next day, he'd walk up and look over my shoulder! He'd turn around and say, "Oh, I forgot! Never mind!" He wrote amazing reviews of my work—his observations were excellent. I read it before he presented it to our boss—the center's director, and I said, "If you put down excellent then I don't have anywhere further to go," and he said, "Okay, I will put down very good . . . very, very good." I started seeing clients in December with the coordinator. He was there to help me better understand the paperwork and treatment plans. I never did care for treatment plans because from my own experience, the plans would change *drastically* from week to week. We based our treatment plans off of the psychologists that we worked with. The psychologist would review our files as they came up for three-month review. I would always do mine last because the coordinator would just zip right through them and sign them. He'd say, "Okay

Geri, what's this patient doing?" I would just tell him whether it fit the treatment plan or not. I wasn't their regular type of counselor who went through a degree program. All I had was personal experience and I developed plans from how I saw it.

I started getting a lot of the difficult clients. The intake worker would say, "Geri, I think you would work best with this client." And a lot of them I did. I remember this one client, a homeless man. He would pick up clothes from here or there. His hair was long. He had a long beard and a hat pulled over his head. He came to me because he wanted to stay sober. I think he had been arrested for drunk driving and was court-ordered to seek treatment. After his term was up, he continued. At the time, we took clients for up to two years. It takes a long time to understand how people come to substance abuse and how to overcome it. I had to go to meetings every day to realize this, to progress with my sobriety. I was so withdrawn from society and I just didn't catch on all that quick.

This guy, he started going to meetings. We usually recommended three times a week, according to what people thought. But I said, "Every day, if you can." I said, "I went two times a day, and there were two meetings a day, and I wasn't working." So he started going two times a day, and his progress was coming along the same lines as mine; it was slow, and he didn't want to talk, and it was hard for him to get acquainted with people. We always recommend getting a sponsor and eventually look for three sponsors. Finally one day he came in, and he said, "I got a phone number." I said, "You mean a person from the meeting who you could call every day?" He said, "Yeah, I think so." So, he did. He started calling. One day he came in, and he was clean-shaven and his hair was cut. Nobody recognized him. I heard the intakes whisper to each other, "That is so and so . . ." He was there for his appointment, and he was getting cleaned up. I remember one morning he said, "Good afternoon" or something like that to the secretary, and she just couldn't believe it.

I asked him to get involved in the activities after being acquainted with his sponsor. He went fishing with his sponsor and probably six other guys. It was cold, like now. And he said that was the first time he had any fun sober, going fishing with these guys, and doing their own cooking, and having fun as a group. So that was a good sponsor for him. I said, "Next thing, plan to go to the New Year's Eve dance." The 12-step program held a huge party for their sponsors and sometimes the children. It's a healthy place to be. I didn't think he would *dare*, but his confidence was strong to where he could go to a big function like that. He called me from the dance and said, "I wanted to let you know that I am here."

After that he continued to go the meetings. He had gotten a job and eventually started work in cleaning the state buildings. He worked there long enough to where he got raises and insurance. So he had long-term employment, *good* employment. He was on time for work. He did a good job there. I knew his supervisor and was keeping tabs on him. I went to a new meeting at North Presbyterian Church, which was probably a mile from Cristo Rey, and I went to that meeting with a lady. I went to the meeting and my client was there. He said, "I want to show you something." So he took me to the parking lot. He said: "See that red truck over there?" It was a sparkling red truck. And he said, "That's mine." He had gotten himself a new car and was making payments on it. And I said, "You know, I think it's time you be on your own. You're going to meetings and made all this progress." Later, I did his review and made that my official determination. Of course, I checked in on him for three months in aftercare, but he was officially discharged. I would see him every now and again. He would call me every once in a while and leave messages at work. "I am still ok." He was one of my first cases. I think of him every once in a while. I think about a lot of people that I had as clients.

Getting Involved with the Community

I always wanted to get involved with the Lansing community. It was always in the back of my mind—something that I wanted to do when I was ready—when I was confident in recovery. So I started getting involved with different committees while working at Cristo Rey. This all started when I helped the executive director of Cristo Rey campaign for city council. He eventually became mayor of Lansing. I would use my time off to campaign door-to-door. I never thought about running for any position myself. I always wanted to be in the background—creating things and helping people. I never wanted to be the main person. It was the same thing with the boards. I never wanted to be president or vice president. I just wanted to be part of the community—part of the background. But I still had influence! I shared my ideas with committees and I always made sure to attend meetings.

I started to get involved with the Lansing Indian community as well. Janice, my cousin, approached me about joining the board of directors. Janice was the director of the center and was on the board of the Michigan Indian Benefit Association. The MIBA oversaw what was going on at the Lansing Indian Center, including finances, planning events, and overseeing elder's gatherings. At that time, there was a lunch for elders twice a week, and activities planned for the rest of the afternoon, up until 5 p.m. There must have been fifteen or twenty elders. It was a large group! Of course, community members would show up for lunch and talk to the elders. For me, it was a good way to be reintroduced to the community. I was outside of it for so long. It was at the lunches where I learned a lot about the different skills the elders had. I watched and I listened. This whole thing reminded me of watching my father do his own crafts. They would make things to be sold as fundraising items. There was an entire room set aside for items that were made by the community.

It was hard to get back into the community because I had been out of it since boarding school. I had no idea what it meant to be me—to be a Native person. But there were these people who had always been around—who knew about community and traditions. I was drawn back. I started to recognize who I was. And the 12-step program helped me with this too. It helped me understand how to approach this process: what I could do, what I couldn't do. I resolved a lot of my history about being Native American and about being poor. Janice helped me with that as well. We would go through the Durant Rolls that have all the names in the history of Odawa families. It was in that book that I found out about my mother's and father's last names and how the spelling changed over time. It's also where I learned that Janice was actually my cousin. We didn't know that before! So that connection, it helped while I continued sobriety—while I started to reconnect with the community. It helped knowing that I had family in Lansing but also where I came from. This is something that I would encourage my Native American clients to do: to find out who they are and where they came from. At the time, the center was close to where I lived. The community center also helped with everything. It was nice to be able to drop by, help answer phones, or be with the elders. They never needed help cooking and that was a good thing! I am such a bad cook! Even now, my daughter or her husband has to taste my chili or corn soup to add the seasoning! The center had the best cooks. There were two women who shared the cooking. They made corn soup and fry bread. Everything that they made was just so delicious.

But the funding started to run out. The board members eventually bought a house and moved the center to a new location. This happens a lot with Native community centers. It had a nice, homey atmosphere. There were a lot of people coming in and a lot of support from other organizations too. I forget who was the mayor at the time, but I remember he came to the center too. With all the other programs that were going on there, there were programs that benefited the community a lot. For example, there was an employment program. There was a substance abuse programs—they were all very needed programs. I actually became a part of the community because I held the 12-step meeting there—once a week, during the evening. We were all really supportive of each other. Some of the members would even stay behind and make sure I got to the car because it would be really late and the neighborhood was kind of scary.

Around that time, I became a member of the central advisory board for the 12-step program. You had to have two years of sobriety to be involved. I was the representative who oversaw the day meetings. Eventually, I was elected the secretary for the meetings. Oh my gosh! For those meetings, my knees shook because there was a big audience. Practically half the state was there. I held that position for a year. I took notes and I had to send out a report once a month. At that time, there wasn't an automatic stamping system. There were just single stamps. And if you tried a wet washcloth, oh brother, what a mess! But that was something. You know what though? Before I got a job at Cristo Rey, I was going to Davenport to be a legal secretary. That experience helped me get through the meetings. Things like this help remind me that it's all connected. After helping my boss campaign for city council, he talked to me about being on the City of Lansing human resources advisory board. He came by to give me a big list of positions to choose from. So, I chose human resources. I was there for ten years until I resigned. A lot of powerful people were on that board. The director of the board designed a really important program for the City of Lansing. She could remember details and numbers without looking at her notes. She was like a computer! It was amazing!

Once a month, my daughter and I shared a car. The City of Lansing meeting was always on a Thursday. I think my daughter had class on Thursday. The director of the board would give me a ride home because she lived near me. I don't recall that I missed many meetings. If they couldn't get enough members, the secretary would always say, "I know I can always count on you, but we couldn't get a quorum, so it's canceled." From there, I met the mayor and joined the city council. One year, we had a hearing in council chambers. It was the first public hearing we had. I think it ended up going until eleven o'clock at night. Everybody had to share their experiences and there was no time limit. So the next hearing, it was quite a bit different. They rang the bell after three minutes and it went a lot smoother. To have the whole community looking up at you . . . I didn't know what to do with anything: my face or hands. I had to just sit there, and it was embarrassing.

But, for another meeting, my daughter was going to drop me off because she had to testify on behalf of Cristo Rey's child services. She was the coordinator. We were getting ready to go and her cat had been sick. She asked me to give the cat some medicine and it clawed me in the head. There were three claws stuck in my head! There was blood running down my face, but I was still ready to go to the hearing! She took me to the sink to clean me up and started laughing. I said, "This is not funny." She said, "Mom, there are three claws in your head." I thought, *Oh no!* We didn't know what to do, so with this towel wrapped around my head, she dropped me off at the hospital. The doctors and nurses were laughing too, these claws sticking out of my head. That was the only time I was ever absent from the board meeting. I was on all of these committees and boards, including the school and eventually the Woodland Indian Community Center's board of directors. We would have an annual review by that national committee that provides standards for hospitals and our substance abuse programs. They were impressed with my volunteer work. Doing all of this community work, I made some important friendships.

My friend, Janis, is a neat lady. I really treasure her friendship. She has always been so supportive of me. I don't get to talk to her as much as I used to. She's always giving me books about American Indians. I like them but I have a hard time reading them. I like murder mysteries. I remember the first time I met her. She was applying to run the Nokomis Center. I was on the leadership board when she interviewed. This is also how I met Susan Applegate Krouse. I didn't vote for her, but she won anyway. She had a lot of education.

Geri with her friend Janis Fairbanks.

After spending time with Janis, I just supported everything that she did for Nokomis. There were a lot of things that needed to be taken care of and considered. She just went ahead and did them. She had so many resources and volunteers in the community to help her. She reestablished a friendship with the Meridian Township. She was such a hard worker and would stay late. I remember being there with her so many times just watching her work and helping her sort papers and inventory. Lansing has an annual Fall Festival and she made sure that Nokomis was a part of it. It was a big success for her. I made the corn soup and it really sold! This made me feel really good, especially since I'm not that good of a cook. They would say, "This is the best corn soup I had in a long time." Nokomis had a sign on the building that was fading. Janis asked the Boy Scouts to repaint it. I was always so amazed at how she could find people who wanted to help our community. She had people develop a garden around Nokomis where they planted Native American plants like sweetgrass. That was one of her last projects. The board decided to let her go. They said she was costing too much money. She was willing to work part-time because she was going to school. I just never understood why they fired her. Why wouldn't you want a person who was going to have another degree in American Indian studies working there? She brought a lot of knowledge and expertise to Nokomis. She had started the Anishinaabeg language program for both the adults and children.

Developing the Native American Recovery Group

While working at Cristo Rey, I started to develop educational programs. I began with alcohol education in 1981. The members in the group were all on probation and had to complete an alcoholic education program. I set up a six-week program. At first, it was slow and then after the first two months, it was just crowded. I would handle twenty people in this small room. And they say, you should never have a group larger than ten! But everyone got along with each other. When I would walk in, I would hear people say things like, "How'd you do this week?" or "How'd your wife do?" They'd always have some kind of friendly gossip going. I could always tell from their conversations that there was improvement and I would note that in their regular report. Then, I found myself creating programs for heroin, cocaine—pills were not as popular as they are now. Not all of my clients made it. One client who was in the heroin recovery group was found dead. I saw him one week and everything was fine and expected to see him for his next appointment. But he never showed up. He was wrapped around the telephone pole near my work. I actually had to pass by the police scene on my way to work. He had a bad dose of heroin. I don't know what happened that he would resort to that after eight years of sobriety. It was hard learning about the people who never made it.

At the time, I didn't know much about heroin and some of the other drugs. I had this one client who eventually came to my Native American Recovery Group. He told the class that he knew more about drugs than I did. I said, "I think you do." So, I gave him an assignment. He was supposed to write an essay on what he knew about other drugs. Then, he was supposed to write his own goals. One of them was about using his knowledge to help other Native Americans. This helped him into recovery. He realized that he wanted to go to Sault Ste. Marie to help Native Americans. I got to see him a few years ago at a protest at the State Capitol. He just jumped off the tour bus. I didn't expect to see him. He saw me and right away came and hugged me. That was a happy moment. I wasn't trying to relate to my clients. I was trying to learn from them—how they were developing while in recovery.

Even though I was on all these boards and committees, I was still working at Cristo Rey. Cristo Rey became overwhelmed by court referrals. At the time, there was a halfway house and people who were court-ordered requested to attend Cristo Rey. They had to check in and out and every place they were going to had a time limit, so they were constantly moving from place to place. We started to develop educational programs to help people find jobs and get long-term support. The classes drew in a lot of people. I developed a few educational programs too—one for Native Americans and one for children. We introduced our school program to the principals and would see who was willing to give us time. A few schools were willing to have substance-abuse programs come to the school. It was a three-day class, one hour per day. In some of the schools, the children were very, very unruly. One time, my partner called in sick on the second day. We were working with fourth graders. The children were under their desks, lying on top of their desks, talking. The teacher was sitting in the back of the room. And I thought, *Oh my gosh, how can you let this happen?* I looked and there was no reaction to the teacher. So I thought, *Well!* I stood up in front of the room and said, "Hey! If you want to have this class, and if you want to learn something about substance abuse, and learn to ask questions, you are going to be quiet." All of sudden it was quiet, and I thought, *Wow! That's all it took?*

So they sat down and listened to the information I gave, and I thought I would end it maybe twenty minutes early. They all started asking questions. A lot of the questions were about Pepsi and Coca-Cola. The kids were noticing a connection between what I was saying about drugs and alcohol and caffeine. At that time, the kids' parents were abusing those colas as well as alcohol. But the children weren't asking for themselves, but for their parents. They noticed how their parents would drink the colas all day long and carry two liters with them. They wanted to know how to approach their parents and it just brought up a whole bunch of things. It made me think that maybe this is why they are unruly. I wrote it on the report that we had to file. It was interesting because their questions got worked into our program.

I started attending workshops on alcohol awareness. I went to a regional conference in Illinois. I had a lot of opportunities to meet with other counselors. I would go to conferences or present about my programs. We had people from Western Michigan—students from there—who specifically asked me to speak. It was a big feather in my cap! There was also a Native American substance-abuse program at Western Michigan. I had gone to the Midwest Institute—that was a requirement for all the counselors in 1980. I went to that one and the Native American one in 1982 or 1983 with the coordinator of the Native American program. The nice thing about the institute was they had a powwow after the banquet. You could join in the drums and bring your regalia. At one point, I had four or five Native American clients at the same time. I asked them if they wanted to start a recovery group for just Native American clients and their families. This was about 1981. And they did! They gave me so much input on the focus of the meetings—what they wanted. After getting involved with the American Indian community, I was more confident with my beliefs as a Native person. So, I started to see connections between the Odawa side and the 12-step program.

We ended up meeting once a week for about six to eight weeks. Each week, we would have a theme or a set of goals. Sometimes they would relate to the 12 steps and sometimes it would be something else. We even had a film series where we would watch documentaries about American Indians. Each week, we would talk about sobriety and recovery but also use the time to learn more about ourselves as Native people. There was one couple who knew so much about American Indian traditions. The husband made some beautiful dream catchers. He and his wife both made them. They always brought fry bread too. She made really good fry bread. A few people made shawls. The shawls were made with original silk thread. We had money designated for making things. One guy showed us how to mix the sand or the dirt and where it came from and how it was made into clay—how you can make a clay pot. We all made a clay pot. I wish I had kept mine, but I gave it away. He showed all of us. He was a member of the group too. We had a famous artist in our community to help us design a logo—if he could stop drinking, he could really be something. He just listened to the group and then put all their ideas in a design before the meeting was over. "Wow, this is what we need." We hoped he would stay with the group, but he decided not to even if it meant that his probation would be revoked.

In the recovery group, we made T-shirts as well. The members picked the color blue because it symbolized serenity and peacefulness. During the meetings, we would go through the medicine wheel and study it. We discussed how and why we followed it. We would use the medicine wheel and make some comparisons to the 12 steps. We talked about how sweating out the alcohol was like going to the sweat lodge and sweating out the poisons. We talked about how it's important to identify the things we did and how it's hard to face. For the third step, we talk about the Creator and God. I had the members follow a native form of the steps. I even had a poster made of the 12 steps in the Ojibwe language. My sponsor once told me to "stay away from people who are not good for you!" She said, "if they are negative, they are not worth it." And you know what, I believed her. A lot of the things she said were right on target. She had twenty years of sobriety at the time. I thought, *Wow, someone with that much sobriety knows what she is talking about.* In the group, clients would bring their children. Even though I was leading the meeting, it was very much client-directed. The clients would come in and share their expertise on things. This was key to the group. We became a big family. I still keep in touch with so many of them, even now. It was really important to me to run this group even after I retired. When I retired, we advertised for a Native American counselor, but there wasn't any. That was a big problem—there were no Native Americans who were doing substance abuse counseling. I had a contact in Grand Rapids. That person wasn't Native American but they wanted to design the group using my experience. But those people never lasted long in those positions because they didn't live our experiences; the group needed a Native person to facilitate.

In my own experience, it seemed like it was always a bad idea to be *Indian.* It was like a stigma, anywhere I went, or with my mother, we were always in the back of the line, or the end of the line. People would crowd in before us. During the war, I remember us always standing in line with coupons for different things like bread. You know, sometimes today I will notice, especially when I am shopping at the mall or a specialty shop, I'll be standing in line and the attendants will wait on other people first. And I will say, "Wait a minute, I was next!" And a lot of times the person that they were motioning to come forward would object and I would step out, and say, "This is what I want." Then, the clerk has no choice; even if there is a negative reaction, they still have no choice. It really irritates me when I see that, and it's something that has always happened in my life, like I told you before, where they wouldn't serve me at the bar. It's just an example of how people see us as insignificant.

More and more, white people are becoming aware of us, but not enough. One of the people in my Native American Recovery Group was a single father. He brought his two sons with him, and they got along really well in the group. I asked one of the boys, "What is one thing you would like to see changed?" He said, "I would like to get more Native American literature in the school library." And the next question was, "How would go about making this happen?" And he said, "I could start with one book," and I said, "That's all you need!" And, this was coming from a fourteen-year-old. I was kind of surprised that a fourteen- or fifteen-year-old would want to keep coming to our group. So I would have to do things in the group that would make things interesting for the younger ones too. They came up with a lot of good ideas and gave their father a chance to see what was going on in their minds—what was important for them. A lot of times, the boys wouldn't even speak at home. So the three of them, in a sense, started recovery together. In my experience, most Native Americans won't ask for help, especially to non-native people. I think that's why our group was so important, because I was a Native American doing the counseling.

The father, he had been fired a lot because of his drinking. When he started recovery, he was working, but the problem was that he didn't want to leave his sons home alone at night. Since he was a line cook, he had to work every night. That was not a good time for teenagers, or *any* children, to be home by themselves like that. He wanted to work on getting his job back. He had worked at the prison in Jackson as a cook. He started at 6:30 in the morning and would be home by 4:30 p.m. It wasn't bad for the kids to be home by themselves for an hour. We found out in group that this was the one thing he wanted to do again, to get his job back. He had to prove that he was in recovery, and they would restore his seniority and get his insurance. So I called the prison because I knew someone from the central advisory board. I called him and asked him what the situation was with this guy, and being fired, and that I was working with him now, and what he would have to do to get an interview and establish himself with Jackson Prison. He gave me a list of like ten things he had to do. If my client was willing to work on them then he could get his job back. Within the year, he had gotten most of them done, and he went for the interview and they hired him, with our recommendations. He had accomplished his goals, and one of his main concerns was his sons being alone at night. He wanted his family to stay together and be healthier. So, he got that job and the recovery group is at night, and he was able to keep coming to group, which he did with his sons. I think about this story a lot and all the people who just needed a little more support or a different kind of support.

The recovery group was a big hit. People kept coming back. It was impressive and encouraging to see them keep coming back. Sometimes, I would borrow films from the Lansing Indian Center. There was one film about Alkali Lake. We watched it so many times! The group was always by referral. Our group kept getting larger because people were telling their neighbors and families. The group became an introduction to them. If they wanted to stay in the group then they would have to go through intake and the whole process. Of course, when we got a new coordinator, she didn't believe in that process. She wanted all the group members to be registered clients. I had a big problem with her. She had all these good credentials! She was from the social work program at MSU, she was an RN. But she wanted to change everything, including how the group was run. I did not agree with that at all because I believed that if you could get them interested then they would be good clients.

One of the other members of the group was coming because she was drinking again. Her husband drank too and they drank just about every day. She got so exasperated about what was going on, she came into counseling on her own. She talked about getting her husband to come in: "No, he didn't believe in that stuff." After she was in recovery for six months, she finally got her husband to come. I remember making decorations in the gym for some festival. He came in for his appointment, and it was in the evening, and he was just slumped in the chair like "I'm here but I don't like it." I said, "Well, then, do you want to help me cut this stuff out?" He took the scissors. He did a good job! He was an artist! You know all of these unexplored talents these people had, and this lady, she didn't believe in that stuff. She would say to me, "You have to be doing that in your off time, and you can't be doing that in your office." I would do it after she was gone for the day. So this guy came in, we were there, it must have been an hour and a half that we were talking, and he was telling me all kinds of stuff. I was cutting away, and we finished these letters. I said, "Do you know what time it is?" He said, "No." I said, "It's around eight o'clock," and he said, "Where did the time go! This was interesting, I will come back next week." The guy is still sober, he and his wife both. The big thing is trying to find a way to reach people—to break through. And you just never know how it happens. Prayer has a lot to do with it too, and your relationship with spirituality and the 12 steps. Understanding what's going on, empathy not sympathy. All kinds of things you learn from the meetings.

Of course, there were a lot of people who struggled or couldn't commit no matter what we tried. They were some of the sad ones. I still think about the client who took some bad heroin and then wrapped himself around a pole. There was also a person in my 12-step group who had twenty-two years of sobriety. He stopped coming to meetings for two days. This was really unusual because he was normally there every day. People were starting to wonder what happened to him. That day after the meeting, a bunch of the guys went over to his house and he was there drunk and helpless because the alcohol really devastated him, you know, after being sober for so long. With sobriety it continues, like, it didn't take much for him to be almost comatose because of the alcohol poisoning. But they got him to the hospital and into treatment. He was there for ten days. He came back to meetings, and I could tell this took a lot for him to start again, especially after twenty-two years of sobriety. He said, "This can happen to anybody. I'm telling my story because it will help you." Oh brother! That was so sad. But then everyone was happy that he made it through. That someone cared enough to find him. This is a part of the service work that goes with recovery. You know, helping people. I saw this happen a lot. I received so much from people in recovery too. One of the members, who we thought was just a regular person, ended up being a minister at one of the churches. He came in one day, really sad like he was in shock. We found out that someone broke into this church and broke all the stained glass. He said, "I just have a hard time going in there to face it and think about how people can be so destructive." After the meeting, I asked how many people would like to come and help me clean up the church gym. A bunch of us went! When he came back the next day, he was so pleased. We were too.

Every once in a while, I still go to meetings. I used to go to the one at Okemos church. But one time, I went with my friend, a Native American man. He has real long hair and he brought a friend with him too. Afterward, I heard some of the people in the meeting and the folks who run the church talking about letting "that" kind of person into the church. And I never went back there, and nobody called me to check in on me. They couldn't care less, you know. That was the closest place to go; at night, I don't drive very far anymore, and that was really close. I just never went back. I could never understand the church being like that, or people in the 12-step program. It's not a part of the steps. You just never know who you could be sitting next to—someone from skid row or like I mentioned, someone from the attorney general's office.

You know, we hear a lot about all of the struggles that African Americans went through, but Native Americans had similar struggles. We're still going through it. We weren't considered first-class citizens when African Americans were allowed to vote. This is our land and we were told that we couldn't vote. I still have a lot of anger. Even after I stopped drinking and my life started getting to be on a good track, I still have those background feelings from when I was growing up. Different thoughts coming to mind, how we're still considered lower-class citizens. Service work helps me manage those thoughts, especially doing work for the Native community. I hope that this book shows that American Indians have done important work in our communities. I have so many amazing American Indian friends.

One of my friends was an Ingham Country commissioner and she was the vice chairwoman for Little Traverse. She and her daughter are so amazing. When my boss became mayor, he asked me about Debbie and if I thought she would make a good assistant. I told him, the one thing that impresses me the most about her is that she is able to say things without hurting other people's feelings; that takes some doing! He said he is considering her and of course, his niece was the mayor's assistant. But that was one thing that she had done, and she was an assistant to the state representatives, two state representatives. I mean, that kind of thing, is where a Native American should be. There are a lot more Native Americans that are getting to be recognized for different things that they are doing. Her daughter is a master plumber and has her master's degree in Teaching English as a Second Language. It just impresses me!

We still have so many struggles in the school system. I'm really impressed by my daughter, though. She's overcome so much. I remember there was this one nun who later became principal of Holy Cross. She told Jan that she was never going to make it, never going to make anything of herself because she didn't know *math!* She was only in fifth grade! Every year, Holy Cross has a school festival and we would go. When Jan graduated high school, we made sure that the nun knew about it. When she completed two associates at LCC, we made sure the nun knew about it. Now, she has her master's degree! The nun was eventually fired. I just can't imagine how many other children she said that to and who took it to heart. When I was doing the educational programs in the school system, I had a couple of teenagers who needed encouragement and care. One of them was in special education. He was told that he was dumb. I thought, *How can a teacher do that?* How can they not encourage? Instead of discourage. So, I got some projects together for the student to show him that he could do something, that he was special. Maybe it wasn't what they wanted him to do, but he could do other things. It's important to show our children that they can do things—that they have abilities, expected or not.

The other student that I remember was a really difficult case. She would smoke marijuana in between classes. I had about three or four sessions with this girl, who was about sixteen years old. And I thought, *I am not making any headway with this girl.* I was just, as they say, warehousing. It was because her parents wanted her to be there and because she was a referral. I noticed that her fingernails were always so dirty or jagged. One day, I said to her, "You know, I am having problems with my fingernails, and I see you are too. How about we just put some nail polish on, file them, and see what happens? That would be your assignment for next week, just get some nail polish and put it on." During our next session, she came in and just sat there like she usually did without saying anything. She put her hands on the desk and said, "I did what you asked me to do." She filed them and put nail polish on—black. But she bit her nails, that was the problem. I said, "Well, next week, let's put on some other kind of nail polish, let's put on a brighter color." That went on for two or three weeks. In the meantime, I would show videos tapes about alcoholism and drug use and we would discuss them. But it seemed like it didn't go *anywhere.* One day, she came to the session and she was beaming. She said that someone had offered her marijuana. She said, "I said no, I said no, thank you." And I was so happy for her, oh my gosh! I got really excited. She said, "That doesn't mean I am going to quit." "But," I said, "at least it's a start!" So after that, there was such a big difference! She even noticed it. She started to go to class and remember her books. She was getting better grades. She still smoked after school. Both her parents worked, so she was home a couple hours by herself. I know one thing she wanted was a cat, and her dad refused to let her have a cat because she was not responsible enough to take care of it. Together, we made an outline of all her responsibilities and that helped convince her parents. She ended up getting the cat and taking such good care of it. She stopped smoking completely. She was getting more trust from her parents. She was going to graduate soon and attend Michigan State. Since her house was so close to the campus, her parents wanted her to live at home, but she desperately wanted to live on campus. Since she made so much progress, they let her. I discharged her and she's been doing great ever since. Every once in a while she would call me. Sometimes, she asked for help on her college assignments and sometimes just to check in. For a while, I got so busy that I lost track of her. Every now and then, I get a card from her just letting me know that she is still doing okay.

PART FOUR

Stories of Healing

Big Changes: Retirement and Contractual Work

I retired from Cristo Rey at the age of sixty-five. I had a new grandson, and I had never started working at Cristo Rey for money. I thought it was a good time to make a change. I was there to help people. The counseling services were changing. It wasn't the same anymore. There was limited budgets and limited time with clients. There were new styles of paperwork and I had to get authorizations for even just one year of counseling. I was used to seeing clients through phases of recovery. We had long-term relationships. It was getting to the point that I could only see the clients two or three times and those visits were *really* just assessments. I thought, due to these drastic changes, it was a good time to retire. Both the coordinator and the executive director wanted me to do some contractual work. So I continued with two classes for a couple of years. It was fun to just come and go. I didn't have to do a whole bunch of stuff. Then, my contractual work came to a close. My office had been all cleared out. It was like I didn't have a home anymore. It had been my home for twenty years. I was sad to let go of this part of my life.

I remember when Cristo Rey was expanding. The educational programs were the first to move over to the new building in the old High Street school. When we moved in, people were still hammering and sawing—taking down walls and adding walls. We were allowed to pick the space we wanted for our office. I picked an office that had a window, so I could open it and smoke! Our offices downstairs were huge classrooms. It was really convenient for me. It had a big fireplace for show and I could set up a table for my classes. At that time, the clients were allowed to smoke during the classes and I just opened the windows and doors. The janitors thought it would be nice for me to have a screen to divide the office. This way, I could have privacy with a client. They could stay and ask questions without everyone watching and listening to them. It worked out pretty good!

Later, the executive director worked with the substance abuse program to make the entire building smoke-free. This meant that I would have to go outside. At the time, I had been praying to stop smoking. So this was just one of those bridges to help me over. Shortly after the new rule, I had surgery. I was in the hospital for a day or so. During that time, I asked the surgeon to look up those smoking patches that had just come out. They aren't on the market anymore, but they worked for me. I took the prescription and the pharmacist knew all about how to quit smoking. He had gone to workshops and gave me all the information. I said, "Well, I haven't stopped yet, but I am thinking about it." I had the prescription and put it in the bathroom and just left it there. One day, I went home and saw I had one cigarette in my pack. Normally I would go out and get a new pack or even a carton, because I used to buy them by the carton.

For some reason, I just never went out. I smoked that last cigarette and there was no panic to run out and get another pack. During the night I woke up and had to go to the bathroom and decided to put that patch on. I thought, *I am going to find out if this going to work.* I woke up about 6:30 and had no desire to smoke. I thought, *Hey, this is OK*; there was no . . . nothing! On the way to work, I usually smoke a cigarette. But I got through a whole day without smoking a cigarette. I thought, *This is really working.* I got Nicoret, the little gums, and quartered them. I thought I would chew a tiny piece if I felt like I needed to smoke. It helped! So whenever I had an urge to smoke, I just went on using a quarter of the cube. This experience helped me design a class on how to quit smoking. I collaborated with a friend of mine, a doctor, and she would help out in the class. She was right there to write a prescription for anyone right there if they wanted to quit. I stopped smoking on February 19, 1990.

There are a lot of friendships from my time with Cristo Rey. We were like a family. We are all hard workers and just people—interested in helping people. The people who weren't never lasted long. The ones who cared were there for years and years. It was amazing just to see that many people in one building. There must have been thirteen or fourteen programs going at the same time. We had a meeting once a week and the whole center would get together. We talked about progress and funding—activities. We would talk about our classes. During those meetings, we would make referrals to each other. A client once said that Cristo Rey was like a non-stop shopping place. They would come for substance abuse and be referred to Michigan Indian Employment and Training or if they had children, children services. Everything was just so useful. The executive director did a good job getting all of those services there and keeping them going! I really liked that place. It was so polished and pretty. They would hang the wreaths that I made over the big doorways. Some of them are still there. I retired in 1997. For my retirement, my family helped organize a huge surprise party. They pretended that they were taking me out to dinner. As we were walking through the restaurant, I thought, *Why are we going there?* I walked into the room and there was all the entire staff. It was so nice . . . I don't know if I cried or not. I probably did! They had a big buffet set up; people came and talked and told funny stories that happened over the years! There were just so many good memories. I was the first person to retire from there.

After I left, the funding for our services dropped out really quick, like a year or so. They were looking for another Native American counselor, but there just wasn't anyone around who would fit the position. We tried to get one of our interns who worked with me in a lot of the classes. He graduated from MSU's social work program. He got along real well with the clients, so they tried to shift him in to my position, but it didn't work out like we thought it would. Being a Native person made the difference. One of the staff quit and got a job with a substance abuse program in East Lansing. It was down to one to two counselors and a coordinator. It was such a drastic change! I think it was lack of money. The city was losing funding. Our program had county funding and some federal funding. I don't remember the breakdown. I used to do that paperwork. I thought, *Oh my gosh!* I knew what they were talking about but I did not want to do it. I thought directing myself was enough. A lot of times, people don't have any idea of what substance abuse is. The goal is to educate with statistics. And you can't count a person who is in recovery as a statistic. They count those who complete the program in six weeks or six months. But they don't follow up with the person after they complete the program. They don't focus on the recovery aspect.

I continued consulting with the Native American Recovery Group. I would have anywhere from five to ten people; this is not including their families. Some would be referred to that class and maybe last a couple sessions and decided it's not what they wanted, or they don't want to stop drinking or stop *using*. But it made it easier to see a Native American. There were a lot of referrals, especially community referrals. People would come to the group and say, "My mom told me to come see you." The community members would often say to people in trouble, "You better go see Geri!" I had contacts from Grand Rapids, Detroit; Mt. Pleasant; all over Michigan. I was probably the only Native American counselor in this area. There were counselors in Detroit or Grand Rapids, but not here. Still not here. The other day, I got a call from someone who was just starting out. They wanted to meet with me and ask questions. I said, "Anytime!" But they probably got so busy and overloaded because I never heard back. Anytime anyone hears of a Native American counselor, they make referrals to me right away.

Under the contractual work, I continued the Native American Recovery Group, but that was about it. It seemed like most of the members knew that I was retiring and would only be around for the group. So they couldn't call me at Cristo Rey and ask questions, which is what they usually did. Since there was no place to transfer to, most families decided that they would just retire with me. Some of the members had been with me for a while—over three years! By that time, they were in good recovery anyway and could manage on their own. If they needed me, they knew they could always call me. The other groups, they were just phased out. If they wanted to continue with their classes or if their probation officer told them to, I would call and make the referrals because it was easier for me to do it.

Before I retired, I referred some clients to the New Day treatment center in the Keweenaw Bay Indian Community. It's really up north. Many lived there and then when they returned to Lansing, they didn't know I retired. They didn't have a support group. Luckily, the secretary who works for New Day used to work with me at Cristo Rey. I told her that they could always call me. Even fifteen years later, I still get a phone call from them once in a while. People from Michigan Indian Employment and Training would refer people to me as well. So, that's retirement! I still see them from time to time. They look good. It's heartwarming to know how they are doing. It isn't policy to allow a client to continue regular contact. But my policy is that if they still need help, they can call me. This is very different from the new policy changes at Cristo Rey right when I retired. But, being able to talk to them every once in a while now is part of the continuing treatment. Even if I don't get paid for it, it's still important to do. It was never about the money. It was always about the community. They are like my children or relatives. I still talk to one of my client's sisters to just see how she is doing. Her husband has stage-four cancer. I remember one time she called and said, "If you want to stop by, I have a case of—no! Don't think that! I have a case of Diet Pepsi!" It's the relationships that have always been important.

The other day, I got a phone call from someone who was in the recovery group. At one point, I counseled the entire family. I hadn't heard from him for almost two years. He and his sons moved to

Tennessee. He was coming to town because one of the children, a little baby girl, had cancer and was going to walk on soon. The grandparents took care of the baby and would drive back and forth to University of Michigan. When the baby died, I was on the phone with the family. That was very sad. For the funeral, they had an outdoor picnic for the family. It was really nice to see a family gathering without drinking. The man—his mother died of cancer. She was an alcoholic too. She was the one who told them to say, "You better see Geri." She was trying to watch out for her family before she passed. She knew they needed help.

Ghost Suppers and Community Politics

I was speaking to my friend Elaine the other day—she handles all the information at Cristo Rey. She told me that the new director of Cristo Rey does not want to host the ghost suppers anymore because he doesn't want people in the building after 5 p.m. I think I am going to call the board of directors and see what they think of that. This decision will really alienate the American Indians and Hispanics in Lansing. They will all be affected by this. In the eighties, I was in charge of getting the space for the ghost suppers. I asked to see if Cristo Rey would do it. At that time, the American Indian centers in the area were closing because of mismanagement or community politics. My cousin was fired from one of the centers. She was responsible for running it. I still don't know why she was fired. She had connections all over the place. The people who fired her were not even from the community and questioned whether my cousin was even American Indian. These types of discussions are not good for our community.

Different people have organized the ghost suppers in the past. I might make some suggestions, like they should have a prayer spoken in Anishinaabe or that they have something to entertain our questions like a speaker. One time, I even suggested Bingo. One year, I asked people from the University of Michigan to come and do a mini-powwow or a big talking circle. Three guys volunteered and did the drums and one danced. They were a very impressive drum circle. I met one of the guys through my daughter because they both went to Michigan State for a while. They gave a little speech about the history of the ghost supper and then they did the fire. We have to get a license from the fire department. My boss said they could have a big grill out there. We had these young men as our firekeepers and they were having fun. It was huge!

A few times, we would have a pipe carrier come to the ghost suppers. He always presented a good ceremony. I've only missed a few of the ghost suppers. It's been difficult to keep people in positions to serve the Native American community. The job doesn't pay very well. I've thought a lot about the ideal ghost supper. People would have name tags or there would be a sign-in sheet with their phone numbers so the organizers could call them next year. There would be a speaker and someone always saying a prayer. And there would be a list of the types of dishes to pass and who will bring them. I don't see too many children at ghost suppers. We need to find more ways to get our children interested. This is something that I've struggled with with my own grandchildren. They do not want to be involved. They used to. I used to make ribbon shirts for the boys and a dress for my granddaughter. I would try to come up with activities to get them interested. One time, the kids went to Traverse City and camped for two nights. They had fun! They learned how to make a bow and arrow and how to cook wild rice. They learned a lot of things. If we could try to get the kids interested in the ghost supper. I think our pipe carrier does a good job explaining what he does. The last time he was here was for my sobriety anniversary. He was like, "You have almost thirty-eight years now!" But that would be my wish.

It's a priority to get the younger generations involved. It's not like when I was a young person and didn't want to get involved. I can't say they are more accepted but they are more recognized as Native Americans. But also, my grandchildren are mixed and are sometimes asked to measure. This makes their identity so complicated. I think it's a rarity that I am full blood. At one time, I was on seven different boards. Now, it seems like I can relax a little during the day. When the children get home, it is time for snacks and dinner and homework. I was asked by the person who is in my old position to sponsor a Native American meeting and those were during the years when I started to stop participating. I thought, *Well, if she is willing to take care of it, I will.* Now she has two meetings, but I don't think the Native Americans really go. I was thinking about letting the responsibility go to another person. Because that's what you do. You take the responsibility of starting the meeting, but you have to let go. You have to let somebody else handle it. You become a guide and see if it isn't going well, you offer a hand.

On My Friends and Support System

I just want to make sure that I have all the people in my life in the story especially where they are all now and how they got there. They have kept me going. They are important to my story of recovery. One of my friends just got married. The ceremony was in the Cooley Gardens and it is beautiful there. I was invited and I regret not going. I really wanted to meet her husband. She has two children from a prior marriage and I wanted to see how the children took to their new father. She finally was able to get the children back. Her mother and father were watching them for a while. I've known this family for a while now. She used drugs and drank alcohol. She straightened her life out and was able to get them back. I'm glad for that—they were able to be a family. The grandparents had a lot of struggles trying to keep the children. They were trying to get them through the Indian Child Welfare Act, through the state. The department was run by a white person. It was such a sad case too.

The people were from our tribe, the Odawas.

The director wanted to place the children with a white family. But the grandparents were ready and they were the grandparents and they had a home where the culture was visible. The director fought so hard to keep the children away from their grandparents. They had a big house and they were a part of a big family. They had to go to probate court. I wrote a letter of recommendation for them. The judge ruled against the family even after the family went to talk to her. The children were placed with a white family that promised to incorporate the Native American aspect. The family thought that going to a powwow was enough. And, they didn't do anything else. Lansing has so many Odawa and American Indians in the area. Our tribe is only a few hours away. Why wouldn't they try to learn more for the children? Since there were so many changes, the grandparents wanted them in counseling with me. The white family only allowed the children to see me like six or seven times. But the grandparents really fought a lot. They went to the tribe and that is how they won the children back. These adoption issues come up all the time. I counsel a lot of families who are going through this process because of the alcoholism.

I was working with another family. Both the parents were in treatment. So their children were put in foster care. The father was Native American and he went to treatment center in the Upper Peninsula. He stayed there for about six months and then moved to a halfway house. He went to meetings every day and made really good progress. The mother was in counseling with me and she wanted to bring the children to come to counseling as well. That was one of their visits. When the children came, it was clear they were not cared for. Their hair wasn't brushed and their clothes were dirty. She was very upset. I helped her brush the children's hair. I sent a report to the social worker and told her that as far as I was concerned, the foster parents weren't being parents. But the Indian child welfare worker wanted the children to stay with that foster family. I don't know what happened to that family. I retired right around that time. I know that the mother stayed in counseling for a long time between her drug use and losing the children—she had a lot of things to work out. She was allowed visitation during counseling and the children were able to come to the recovery group for the sessions dedicated to the potluck and family issues. I supervised the visitations and it was just really sad. They never wanted to leave their mother.

I've talked about my friend—the ex-marine—a lot. He was the one who encouraged me to get a job at Cristo Rey. His daughter called the other day. She's a forest ranger at Alcatraz. We still talk fairly often. If she's ever in town or passing through, we'll try to see each other. When she went to Grand Valley State University, she used to come over on her way to see her mother. It's funny how she stuck so close. When she was growing up, she kind of considered me her second mother. She would always come around when she was here. She would take me to a meeting with her. I used to babysit her when she was a little girl. I remember one incident when she was about five years old. Her mom would get mad at her for different things. One time, she tipped over a plant and kept saying, "I'm sorry, I'm sorry." I would say, "I'm sorry is enough; let's clean this up. Now, we'll have to plant the plant over again." Once, she told me, "I will always remember that. You are always so understanding." I think about her a lot and how she survived witnessing the alcoholism of her father. She would take me to meetings and would go to Alanon. I don't know how my daughter ever escaped all this turmoil. I introduced her to Alateen and Alanon, but it wasn't for her. She graduated from Lansing Community College and attended Michigan State for a while until she transferred to the University of Michigan. After she moved back to Lansing and got married and had children, she went back to Michigan State and got her master's degree. When she was a little girl, she was always so shy and withdrawn. Now when you see her, she has so much confidence. I think it's a point of pride for her to have these children. She and her husband take such good care of them. There will not be any question between them on who takes care of them. They always back each other up.

I found out a month ago that a friend of mine died of a heart attack. He was my boss's nephew. I didn't even know about it! It was such a shock. He was a lot younger than me, by twenty years maybe. He was a janitor at Cristo Rey when I worked there. He was always so nice. He'd let us use the gym for the ghost suppers. Ordinarily, they would charge for groups, especially since they needed a staff person there. After the ghost suppers, he would always say, "I'll lock up. I'll take care of it." When I worked there, he would always watch out for me. A lot of times, I would have to work real late. And he would always stick around. I would be like, "I'm ready to go." And he would say, "I'm coming, Geri!" He always did that. He would check all the doors to make sure. I would have classes late at night and there would be multiple entrances for him to check. I remember him from the first time I was hired and he was pushing the broom through the hallway. When we moved into the new building, he helped me pick out my office—the one with a window because I smoked. I had it all decorated with plants. One of my male clients said, "If I ever have an office—I want one like this." I am still so sad about my friend's passing.

My Grandchildren

When I retired, I was still living by myself. I lived in this place that was so run-down. The neighborhood was turning into a drug neighborhood. I would get these phone calls. I don't know how they got my phone number—probably from the phone book. But it was scary. They were like, "I can see you . . . I know what time you get home." Nothing ever happened, but it was threatening. I moved in with some friends from the 12-step program for a while. Then, my daughter would call or she would have her son call—he must have been two or three years old at the time. He would say, "Mommy wants you to come over and have some coffee," or "Mommy put some coffee on for you." It was very subtle! I would come over and she would go to work or play tennis or run errands. It would take me about twenty minutes to get to that side of town and I babysat two or three times a week. Sometimes, it would get to be too late or my daughter had something to do the next day and I would stay overnight. So, that's how I came to live with them. Taking care of my grandchildren—it's a job that I really like.

Oh my gosh! The grandchildren, they keep me busy. One day, I was writing the errands that I had to do, let me see: the oldest had tennis so he was going right to court from school, so I was to pick him up at 4:30 and pick up the children at 3:30 and go pick up my grandson because he had play practice after school at 5 and at 6:15 his tutor would come for his violin lesson. They have a mentoring student music program at Okemos High School for six sessions. So this was all in one day. My son-in-law looked at me and said, "Maybe I should go to Lamai's for dinner." So I didn't have to fix his dinner. It's the place where my daughter and son-in-law met. At that time, my daughter and I shared a car because she would go back and forth to the University of Michigan for classes. We would stop there every once in a while and have supper. Lamai, the owner, is from Thailand. She serves the best Thai food. One day, we stopped and he was there. So, when Lamai was checking us out, she introduced them. She is so funny. She asks my daughter, "What's your phone number?" And she put it on a sticky note and stuck it on his motorcycle jacket and she said, "You call her, you go out, you go have dinner here." And they did!

So, with three children, it's really interesting because they have so many things to do, so many activities. Some of the mothers know me, the teachers, the principals—especially the secretary at school. She said, "You are a great grandmother." I would come to the school carrying a violin for my youngest grandson or my grand-daughter would call, saying, "I have wet socks, could you bring me a pair of dry socks?" The secretary would ask me, "Do you want me

Geri and her granddaughter, Emilia, on her seventh birthday.

to do it or do you want to do it?" I could see that she was busy and would take the socks or whatever they needed to the classroom. The school was going to do an international festival and they asked me if I want to do something. I had done this festival before and all the people who helped me were all gone. I didn't know what to tell them. I did write down that I would make corn soup like I did last year and maybe make a display of regalia and jewelry. We can make bracelets with colorful beads.

Getting Older

I've been consulting with Michigan Employment and Training for over ten years. I liked it because I could set my own schedule. So I could be home when the grandkids went off to school. But then, I started to want to be here if they called and needed something. They always do. Like, if my granddaughter needs something for Girl Scouts. Right now, they are making dresses for little girls in Africa. I have a coworker who sends me cards on my birthday and anniversaries for sobriety. She is the one who is legally blind. I can't believe she puts that much effort into a friendship and writes a card. She always writes these little messages, like encouraging positive thinking. She is one great friend. One time, I drove us to lunch and turned down a one-way street. I said to her, "I'm glad you can't see what's going on right now!" The traffic was coming right at us! I had to laugh. I told her what was going on. She said, "Geri, see if I go to lunch with you anymore!" But I talked to her yesterday. There are so many things we have in common, like getting old. She said, "Geri, I can't hold onto things anymore." I lost my grip too. I said, "I couldn't pull off the top of a marker. I had to ask my grandson and he just pulled it off!" She said, "Well, that makes him feel like he's growing up. He's strong." I never thought of that, I just thought about getting the top off before I forgot the information. My memory is okay at times. It comes and goes. Sometimes, I am nervous about whether or not I can recall stories. I have a hard time remembering names, but I know their phone numbers and where they are working. I hop from stories to stories. But boy! It will just slip my mind when I go from one room to another.

About five years ago, I started thinking about going back to work. I tried to talk myself into starting a women's domestic violence education group. One of my friends does this work. She told me she would help me—we would share materials. I called an advocate about it. I remembered her from when she gave a talk at my Native American Recovery Group. She was just starting out then. I asked her, "How do I go about starting a domestic assault group?" She said, "Right here!" She would oversee the group. I thought, *That sounds so inviting.* But then, I told her later, "Let me think about it. If I call back, I'll give you my availability." I was a little younger then. I decided not to and keep doing grandma care.

All of this makes me think of my daughter, her husband, and the children. They all spend so much time together. They do things together as a whole family. I've thought a lot about where I used to live and the difference of where I live now, with my daughter,

Geri's family portrait (from left): Chase, Emilia, Geri, Traverse, Rob, and Jannus.

son-in-law, and the kids and the way I lived with my parents or with my husband. One of the differences is that when my husband and I used to drink, there was so much stuff that happened. And, to be in this house . . . It's just so *quiet* here. There's no throwing things around, like my ex-husband and I used to do. No late-night arguing. My ex-husband used to work nights. And some nights, I would wonder about what would happen when he came home. I think that's why I drank like I did. I knew that when he got home, it would be stormy whether I was drinking or not. The alcohol was numbing. When I would hear that car pull in the driveway, I always wondered what would happen. If he would be gone for good or what he would be like when he came home. He couldn't care less what he did when he came home. It's just so much different here. It's a lot more peaceful. It was the way I was hoping retirement would be.

Epilogue

It's been five months since Geri walked on. Her family holds a memorial on May 19, 2019. It includes all of her favorite things: friends and family, a backyard with lush plants and trees, a feast and giveaway, a ceremony around a fire, and good stories with a lot of laughter. The pipe carrier, the son of the pipe carrier who conducted Geri's naming ceremony and Susan's memorial, is tending to the fire and encouraging us to come and sit down. Geri's grandchildren are pretty much grown now. They are on the next stage of their journeys and reflect the love, care, and nurturing of their parents, grandmother, and community.

After the ceremony, the pipe carrier invites us to take turns sharing stories about Geri. We're encouraged to tell funny stories—happy stories to let Geri know that she can leave us, and to carry on her journey. Her passing is still raw for many of us, and we struggle to follow this advice. As I listen to her friends and family talk about Geri, I start to associate faces with the stories she's told about her support system. This is what I share when it's my turn to speak: I let them know that Geri told me about their friendships and experiences because these relationships gave Geri purpose—these relationships became a path for her recovery and healing.

When we decided on the structure of this book, Geri was insistent on ending with that last paragraph about retirement. She wanted us to know that she had the life she always wanted and how grateful she was for her daughter, son-in-law, and grandchildren. This is the story she wanted us—all of us—to have before she left us. I've listened to Geri's stories so many times. As I prepare this book for publication, I am left with her words about retirement, service, and the significance of young people being encouraged to continue the work. I am no longer the twenty-five-year-old graduate student looking to understand her place in the world. Geri has provided that guidance for me as well. Now, I am a mother to my own strong and brave children and an aunty to so many Indigenous youth. It's my turn—our turn—to do the work Geri spent her life doing: to care for our communities, to learn our teachings, to spend time with elders, to tend to our bodies and minds, to listen and learn from our mistakes, and to keep trying at that corn soup until we get it right.

Miigwetch for listening,
Andrea Riley Mukavetz (May 2019)

Works Cited

Absolon, Kathleen (Minogiizhigokwe). 2011. *Kaandossiwin: How We Come to Know.* Winnipeg: Fernwood Publishing.

Anderson, Kim. 2011. *Life Stages and Native Women: Memory, Teachings, and Story Medicine.* Winnipeg: University of Manitoba Press.

Austin, Brenda. 2013. "Same-Sex Marriage Is A-OK With Little Traverse Bay Bands." *Indian Country Today* (April 19, 2013). https://indiancountrytoday.com/archive/same-sex-marriage-is-a-ok-with-little-traverse-bay-bands (accessed September 9, 2021).

Blackbird, Andrew. 1900. *The Indian Problem, from the Indian's Standpoint.* Ypsilanti: The Scharf Tag. Label & Box Co.

Blackbird, Andrew. 1887. *History of Ottawa and Chippewa Indians of Michigan.* Ypsilanti: Ypsilanti Printing House.

Benton-Banai, Edward. 2010. *The Mishomis Book: The Voice of the Ojibway.* Minneapolis: University of Minnesota Press.

Brooks, Lisa. 2008. *The Common Pot: The Recovery of Native Space in the Northeast.* Minneapolis: University of Minnesota Press.

Childs, Brenda J. 2000. *Boarding School Seasons: American Indian Families, 1900-1940.* Lincoln: University of Nebraska Press.

Erdrich, Louise. 2003. *Books and Islands in Ojibwe Country: Traveling Through the Land of My Ancestors.* National Geographic Directions.

Ettawageshik, Frank. 1999. "My Father's Business." In *Unpacking Culture: Art and Commodity in Colonial and Postcolonial Worlds,* edited by Ruth B. Phillips and Christopher B. Steiner, 20–29. Oakland: University of California Press.

Fox, Emily. 2013. Northern Michigan tribe legalizes same sex marriage. Michigan Radio, NPR.

Gould, Janice. 1992. "The Problem of Being 'Indian': One Mixed-Blood's Dilemma." In *De/Colonizing the Subject: The Politics of Gender in Women's Autobiography*, edited by Sidonie Smith and Julia Watson, 81–87. Minneapolis: University of Minnesota Press.

Harjo, Joy. 1996. "Perhaps the World Ends Here." In *The Woman Who Fell from the Sky: Poems*, 68. London: W. W. Norton & Company.

Jones, Jennifer, Dee Ann Bosworth, and Amy Lonetree. 2011. *American Indian Boarding Schools: An Exploration of Global Ethnic & Cultural Cleansing*. Mt. Pleasant: Ziibiwing Center of Anishinaabe Culture & Lifeways.

Krouse, Susan Applegate, Andrea Riley Mukavetz, Leanne Silvey. "Talking Circles with Multi-generational Odawa Women." February 2009.

Little Traverse Bay Band of Odawa Indians. 2005. *Our Land and Culture: A 200 Year History of Our Land Use*. http://ltbbodawa-nsn.gov. Last modified 2014.

Lobo, Susan. 2003. "Urban Clan Mothers: Key Households in Cities." *The American Indian Quarterly* 27, no. 3&4 (summer/fall): 505–522.

Lomawaima, K. Tsianina, and Teresa L. McCarty. 2006. *"To Remain an Indian": Lessons in Democracy from a Century of Native American Education*. New York: Teachers College Press.

Million, Dian. 2014. *Therapeutic Nations: Healing in an Age of Indigenous Human Rights*. Tucson: University of Arizona Press.

Our Land and Culture: A 200 Year History of Our Land Use. 2005. Harbor Springs, MI: Little Traverse Bay Bands of Odawa Indians.

Powell, Malea. 1999. "Blood and Scholarship: One Mixed-Blood's Story." In *Race, Rhetoric, and Composition*, edited by Keith Gilyard, 1–16. New Hampshire: Heinemann-Boynton/Cook Publishers.

Powell, Malea. 2002. "Listening to ghosts: An Alternative (Non) Argument." In *ALT DIS: Alternative Discourses and the Academy*, edited by Patricia Bizzell, Chris Schroeder, and Helen Fox. 11-22. Portsmouth: Heinemann-Boynton/Cook Publishers.

Powell, Malea. 2018. *Stories Take Place: A Native Rhetoric Manifesto.* Unpublished manuscript.

Riley Mukavetz, Andrea. 2021. "Baskets, Birchbark Scrolls, and Maps of Land: Indigenous Making Practices as Oral Historiography," in *The Arts of Indigenous Health and Wellbeing,* edited by Nancy Van Styvendale, J.D. Mcdougall, Robert Henry, and Robert Alexander Innes, 49-72. Winnipeg: University of Manitoba Press (forthcoming).

Simpson, Leanne Betasamosake. 2014. "Land as Pedagogy: Nishnaabeg Intelligence and Rebellious Transformation." *Decolonization: Indigeneity, Education & Society* 3, no. 3: 1–25.

Simpson, Leanne Betasamosake. 2017. *As We Have Always Done: Indigenous Freedom through Radical Resistance.* Minneapolis: University of Minnesota Press.

Smith, Linda Tuhiwai. 1999. *Decolonizing Methodologies: Research and Indigenous Peoples.* London: Zed Books.

Wilson, Shawn. 2008. *Research Is Ceremony: Indigenous Research Methods.* Winnipeg: Fernwood Press.

Womack, Craig. 1999. *Red on Red: Native American Literary Separatism.* Minneapolis: University of Minnesota Press.